1953/54
WEST BROMWICH ALBION

The 1953/54 squad. From left to right, back row: Arthur Fitton (Trainer), Eph Smith (Secretary), Vic Buckingham (Manager), Alan Everiss (Assistant Secretary). Second row: Stan Rickaby, Joe Kennedy, Jimmy Dugdale, Ray Barlow, Jimmy Sanders, Jimmy Dudley, Len Millard, George Lee, Norman Heath. Third row: Mr L. Pritchards, Mr S.R. Shepherd, Mr W.H. Thursfield (Vice-Chairman), Major H. Wilson Keys (Chairman), Mr J.W. Gaunt jnr (Director), Mr T.W. Glidden (Director). Front row (on ground): Reg Ryan, Ronnie Allen, Johnny Nicholls, Frank Griffin.

1953/54
WEST BROMWICH ALBION

Tony Matthews

TEMPUS

*To all the players who performed so wonderfully
well for West Bromwich Albion FC in 1953/54.*

First published 2004

Tempus Publishing Limited
The Mill, Brimscombe Port,
Stroud, Gloucestershire, GL5 2QG

© Tony Matthews, 2004

The right of Tony Matthews to be identified as the Author
of this work has been asserted in accordance with the
Copyrights, Designs and Patents Act 1988.

British Library Cataloguing in Publication Data.
A catalogue record for this book is available from the British Library.

ISBN 0 7524 3124 2

Typesetting and origination by Tempus Publishing Limited
Printed in Great Britain by Midway Colour Print, Wiltshire

Acknowledgements

I would like to say a sincere thank you to the following people who have helped in the production of this special anniversary book: to James Howarth and colleagues at Tempus Publishing; to Dr John Evans (secretary of West Bromwich Albion FC); to my good friend Colin Mackenzie (Solihull Lodge); to fellow historians/statisticians Paul Joannou (Newcastle United), Graham Hughes (Wolverhampton Wanderers), Dennis Clarebrough (Sheffield United) and John Crooks (Cardiff City); to Steve Cork and Ruth Hickman (Sandwell & District Council) and to Robert Hazel (Sandwell Central Library).

I would also like to thank eight members of the 1953/54 playing squad, namely: Ray Barlow, Wilf Carter, Jimmy Dugdale, Frank Griffin, Stan Rickaby, Jimmy Sanders, Ronnie Allen and Johnny Nicholls (all of whom were very good friends) and the club's former secretary and director Alan Everiss and former physiotherapist Fred Pedley, who either loaned or given me photographs over the years.

Thank you as well to the many Albion supporters who have sent or loaned me pictures, newspaper cuttings, scrapbooks etc. at odd times.

Last, but by no means least, I say a huge thank you to my darling wife Margaret who, I know, at times has had to endure an awful lot from me as I've worked away on the keyboard with programmes, pictures, books and other Baggies memorabilia scattered all over the floor.

Tony Matthews

Pride of the Black Country

Fifty years ago, in 1953/54, West Bromwich Albion, in the minds of a lot of people, had their greatest season ever – coming so very close to completing the coveted double by winning the FA Cup and finishing runners-up in Division One to neighbours Wolverhampton Wanderers. During the campaign they were referred to, on many occasions, as 'the team of the season', producing a brilliant style of football which was attractive, full of movement, concise and above all a joy to watch for most of the time! The team had a few hiccups here and there but, generally speaking, under the shrewd and intelligent management of Vic Buckingham, played splendidly and in the end the Baggies were unlucky not to have won the League to go with their Cup triumph.

Albion began their League programme with some excellent displays, especially away from home, and they dropped only two points out of the first eighteen, climbing to the top of the table where they stayed until three weeks before Christmas. They carried on their impressive form after the festive period and, in fact, were only toppled from the top perch twice before having a disastrous run-in (recording only two wins from their last ten matches) that ultimately cost them the title.

Without doubt the team's outstanding performance was a truly magnificent 7-3 League win at Newcastle (after which they were cheered off the field); they later defeated the Geordies 3-2 in a thrilling cup tie at The Hawthorns. Albion also produced impressive home League performances when beating Cardiff City 6-1, Chelsea 5-2, Huddersfield Town 4-0, Tottenham Hotspur 3-0 and for part of the game when clipping Liverpool 5-2. They suffered heavy away defeats at Blackpool, Chelsea and Aston Villa, but were certainly unlucky, in some respects, to have lost both matches against Wolves (each by a single goal) and were certainly hard done by when losing at Bolton and Sunderland.

In the cup, after overcoming a tough encounter in the opening round against Chelsea, Albion knocked out Rotherham United comfortably 4-0, Newcastle United 3-2 in a thriller at The Hawthorns and Spurs, brilliantly, 3-0 before having a battle royal with Staffordshire rivals Port Vale in the semi-final at Villa Park, coming though 2-1 thanks to Ronnie Allen's second half penalty kick winner.

Injuries certainly affected team performances at crucial times. Goalkeeper Norman Heath was seriously injured at Sunderland and right-back Stan Rickaby, initially hurt in the sixth round FA Cup tie with Spurs, aggravated his injury in the semi-final. Both were forced to end their season early – at a time when Albion were flying along. The duo had played wonderfully well, but with them out of the side, Albion struggled and lost four of their last six matches.

But encouraged by what had gone on earlier in the season, and with great determination and willpower, the players pulled themselves together and produced one magnificent effort at

Wembley Stadium where they beat Preston North End 3-2 to lift the FA Cup for the fourth time and so make up for the huge disappointment of missing out on the League title.

Heath, prior to his injury, had played very well. His deputy, Jimmy Sanders, was perhaps too nervous at times in the League games but produced an outstanding display in the cup final. Rickaby was strong and aggressive, while captain Len Millard at left-back was as resilient and consistent as ever. He never had a bad game and neither did Scotsman Jimmy Dudley, who produced some terrier-like performances at right half. Young Jimmy Dugdale played competently throughout the campaign and was often regarded as Albion's best defender. Joe Kennedy, who had his injury problems from time to time, was as calm, cool and calculating as ever. Ray Barlow had a wonderful season, his long, raking passes causing defenders up and down the country all sorts of problems. Frank Griffin, fast and direct with skills to match, made his mark in several games and laid on plenty of chances for strikers Allen and Nicholls while grabbing the most important goal of the season himself (at Wembley). Reg Ryan worked like a Trojan in midfield, grafting hard and long, making chances for his colleagues and scoring a few goals himself in the process. Ronnie Allen was outstanding, recognised by some as the best centre forward in England. He scored some memorable goals and was a constant threat to defenders from day one. If there had been such an award, he would surely been voted Albion's 'Player of the Season'. His partner up front, Johnny 'On The Spot' Nicholls, was a success from the start, producing some quite superb displays and scoring some marvellous and vitally important goals. George Lee, as always, was determined and competitive and he too laid on plenty of chances for his fellow forwards while claiming a few goals for himself.

Fifty years ago Albion came so close to becoming the first team in the twentieth century to complete the League and Cup double. Over the following pages you can read all about their success, how they almost created history and how they won the FA Cup.

Manager Vic Buckingham with future director and vice-chairman Tom Silk.

Pre-season news and round-up

During the summer of 1953 Albion underwent a short, interesting and successful tour to Eire where they won both games, beating a Waterford Select XI 5-4 and a Bohemians Select XI 5-1. They were invited to return any time it was possible. Incidentally a 'fine young Irishman' by the name of Stanley Matthews played against them on each occasion but found, as usual, left-back Len Millard far too good for him!

Ray Barlow travelled to South America with the FA party whilst Joe Kennedy spent the summer training, attempting to get himself fully fit and into shape following a niggling and tedious injury to his right knee that had kept him out of action since February.

Back home, quite a bit of work was carried out at The Hawthorns. New gangways were cut into the terracing behind both goals and into the Handsworth embankment (the popular side, opposite the Halfords Lane stand). The roof of the stand over this part of the ground was blessed with a new waterproof material to prevent the rain from seeping through onto spectators and the steelwork was repainted all round while interior decorating was also carried out. The Hawthorns pitch had its usual intensive treatment to eradicate entirely the signs of the previous season's football and for small sections was completely reseeded.

Some cricket was played, manager Vic Buckingham and Ray Barlow both turning out for West Bromwich Dartmouth's first team and Billy Brookes for the Second XI. Three annual matches were played with the small red ball, Albion beating Aston Villa in a fixture organised for press charities and losing to Dartmouth while gaining a creditable draw with Old Hill CC. Several players, including Ronnie Allen, entered the Professional Footballers' Golf Championship. Unfortunately none of them performed too well and failed to qualify for the final round, Allen being the best-placed Albion star. With Johnny Nicholls, he also backed Pinza, ridden by Gordon Richards, to win the Epsom Derby. Allen, skipper Len Millard and Stan Rickaby all combined business with pleasure during the summer and did some coaching at various seaside resorts.

The Birmingham County FA invited three players – Frank Griffin, Reg Ryan and Allen – to travel with the party to play the Hamburg Football Association in Germany. Ryan sadly had to pull out at the last minute owing to a bout of tonsillitis and was replaced by Ken Hodgkisson. Only Griffin played in the game. Albion's vice-chairman Mr W.H. Thursfield and club secretary Eph Smith were in the official party which travelled to Germany.

Pre-season training commenced in earnest on 15 July 1953, brought forward by two weeks owing to the early start of the League campaign. And among the new faces at the club were centre forward Derek Kevan and full-back Harry Haddington, both signed from Bradford Park Avenue, and winger Freddie Cox who arrived from Tottenham Hotspur where he had played in front of his manager Buckingham. Bill Gallier was upgraded to the

Fred Pedley (Physiotherapist) and Vic Buckingham (Manager) inspecting The Hawthorns' pitch.

professional ranks. A handful of players moved on – Peter Hilton went to Swindon Town, Pat Hewson to Gateshead, George Corbett to Workington, Percy Anderson to Stockport County and Arnold Charlesworth to Rotherham United.

During the build-up to the 1953/54 season manager Vic Buckingham and trainer Arthur Fitton took the players to the famous tonic brine baths at Droitwich where the stiffness which some had developed quickly disappeared. After some vigorous training sessions, the annual public practice match was staged at The Hawthorns on Saturday 15 August. A crowd of almost 4,500 turned out to see the 'Reds' (featuring the first team forward line) beat the 'Stripes' (which included the senior defence) by 8 goals to 2 (it was 5-1 at half-time). In-form Johnny Nicholls (4), Ronnie Allen (2) and Ken Hodgkisson (2) scored for the 'Reds' while Derek Kevan and Wilf Carter replied for the 'Stripes'. A fit-again Joe Kennedy came through the whole ninety minutes unscathed. A total of £3,216 was taken in gate money and duly distributed among local charities.

Prior to the opening game against Arsenal, the reigning League champions and favourites to win the title again, it was announced that there were still a few season tickets at six guineas available for the seating area in the Smethwick End/Halfords Lane corner stand, and also that tickets were on sale, via the club, for the prestigious England v. Hungary international match to be played at Wembley on 25 November 1953. They were priced between 5s and 3s 6d each.

As the hours ticked by prior to the start of the new season, studious Albion manager Vic Buckingham was left with two major selection problems before the game against the Gunners. Who should he utilise at inside right in place of tonsillitis victim Reg Ryan, and should he gamble on a not fully fit Jimmy Sanders in goal? The latter had hurt his wrist in training on the Monday morning and was struggling to move his fingers fluently. In the end the boss chose Nicholls ahead of Wednesbury-born Carter to play in the forward line and decided to select Norman Heath in goal.

GREAT START AGAINST THE CHAMPIONS

Date: Wednesday 19 August 1953
Location: The Hawthorns
Attendance: 41,812

Match title: League
Referee: Mr B.M. Griffiths (Newport)

The biggest League crowd at The Hawthorns for seven months – almost 42,000 – welcomed the players onto the field for the opening game of the season, and it was Albion, attacking the Smethwick End, who looked the more determined in the early stages, making Arsenal's Welsh international goalkeeper Jack Kelsey earn his money with some teasing centres from both flanks.

Indeed it was Kelsey, with two excellent saves, who prevented first Ronnie Allen and then Johnny Nicholls from giving Albion the lead. With Ray Barlow driving forward from the centre of the field and Allen leading the front line superbly, Albion, in between the showers, were yards quicker than the Gunners and after two more close shaves, in the twenty-fourth minute, the lively Nicholls chased a long ball deep into the Arsenal half of the field. He got in front of centre half Bill Dodgin and as Kelsey came out to meet him, neatly slipped the ball between the keeper's legs, ran round and lashed it into the net. A fine individual goal – one Nicholls and Albion thoroughly deserved!

Soon afterwards George Lee should have made it 2-0 while at the other end Cliff Holton forced a fine save from Norman Heath in one of the Gunners' rare attacks.

Albion held sway for long periods and only two brilliant saves by Kelsey prevented them from increasing their lead.

Early in the second half Allen and then Ken Hodgkisson both had chances, and at the other end of the field the former Walsall player Doug Lishman found himself in space but lacked power with his shot.

Albion sewed up the points when, on fifty-one minutes, Nicholls scored another smart goal after some decisive build-up play involving half-a-dozen players, the ball eventually flying past keeper Kelsey after taking a slight deflection off full-back Joe Wade. As Arsenal faded completely, Vic Buckingham's men were denied further goals by the excellence of Kelsey between the posts for the Londoners. It was one-way traffic from the hour mark until full time, as Albion streamed forward in search of more goals. Barlow and Nicholls both had splendid games as did the two Jimmys, Dudley and Dugdale. Allen's passes to both wings were struck with pinpoint accuracy and Heath, although rarely troubled, pulled off fine saves at crucial times during the game.

One newspaper reporter stated that 'Arsenal were tame' and that 'Dodgin will have to improve greatly to retain his place in the side.' As for Albion, he wrote that 'They have a team of fine players. They will be hard to beat, especially at home. "Man of the Match" was without doubt Jack Kelsey ... If it hadn't been for him, Albion would have won by at

Albion 2
Nicholls (2)

Arsenal 0

least four or five goals.' The *Birmingham Gazette* raved about Albion's performance: 'The League champions were soundly beaten and the two-goal margin did not do full justice to the winners.'

Wolverhampton Wanderers started their League programme with a 4-1 defeat at Burnley. Albion two points up!

Club News

Before the second game of the season, Albion's reserve wing half Tim Rawlings, who had gone down with appendicitis, was given the all-clear to start light training. Irish international Reg Ryan was likewise given permission to resume playing following his bout of tonsillitis, although his throat was still sore.

The swelling around goalkeeper Jimmy Sanders' wrist was still prominent and Joe Kennedy was preparing to play for the Second XI against Bolton at Burnden Park on Saturday.

Meanwhile, manager Vic Buckingham, delighted with the performance against Arsenal, had no hesitation in naming an unchanged team for the visit of Bolton, Albion's second game.

George Lee and Ronnie Allen anticipating an excellent season.

Albion: Heath; Rickaby, Millard; Dudley, Dugdale, Barlow; Griffin, Hodgkisson, Allen, Nicholls, Lee.

Arsenal: Kelsey; Wade, Smith; Forbes, Dodgin, Mercer; Roper, Logie, Holton, Lishman, Marden.

A HARD-EARNED POINT

Date: Saturday 22 August 1953
Location: The Hawthorns
Attendance: 29,122

Match title: League
Referee: Mr F.B. Coultas (Hull)

Bolton, beaten 4-3 by Blackpool in the 1953 FA Cup Final, did not play on the Wednesday evening and they came to The Hawthorns for their first game of the season full of confidence after a decent build-up. But they were missing England centre forward Nat Lofthouse (injured) and left-back Tommy Banks.

The game itself proved to be a very scrappy affair and during the opening ten minutes passes went astray from both sides. Bolton's strong-tackling defenders seemed to unsettle the smaller and certainly more fragile Albion forwards and twice in quick succession Johnny Nicholls was fouled from behind. There was a lot of negative football and neither goalkeeper was troubled unduly, Allen firing wide and over for Albion while Bolton's best efforts in the first half came from Harold Hassall (a powerful header which Norman Heath tipped over) and Willie Moir. There seemed a marked improvement in the play of both sides as the second half got going, and after a handful of moderate attacks had petered out Bolton took the lead in the fifty-fourth minute. Albion's defenders got themselves in a tangle as the ball was played down their left flank. Len Millard lost his position, allowing Johnny Wheeler, Bolton's right half, to get to the byline with Johnny Nicholls of all people trying to stop him. He whipped over a low cross that Moir, hovering on the edge of the six-yard area, buried beyond Heath with a well-struck shot.

Albion hit back strongly but found Hanson in the Wanderers' goal equal to anything they threw at him – that is until Ray Barlow climbed highest to head home the equaliser on sixty-three minutes. Stan Rickaby won a free-kick on the right side of the Bolton penalty area, and the ball was driven strongly into the heart of the Bolton defence. After Hanson had punched the ball away from Barlow, Ken Hodgkisson lobbed it back into the goalmouth where Barlow, readjusting himself, got up to steer the ball home.

Allen, who had to stand up to a lot of buffeting from Malcolm Barrass, gave Nicholls a chance but Hanson was in the right spot to save, and soon afterwards Heath saved at the feet of Cobb. Hodgkisson then missed from close range after a Lee cross while at the other end Heath did well to stop a header from Moir.

Albion had the last chance of the afternoon, but Allen miscued from close range and even then the well-positioned Lee scuffed the rebound wide. Barrass had a fine game at the heart of the Bolton defence while skipper Millard was the pick of a disappointing Albion side.

Wolves won 4-0 away at Manchester City to stay two points behind Albion in the chase for League glory.

Albion 1
Barlow

Bolton Wanderers 1
Moir

Club News

As Albion struggled against Bolton and the reserves were losing 1-0 at Burnden Park, so the cricketers of West Bromwich Dartmouth were engaged in a vital end-of-season game with Stourbridge. As a result of their victory West Bromwich Dartmouth duly won the Birmingham League championship for the first time since 1948. This brought immense pride to Albion's vice-chairman W.H. Thursfield JP and director J.W. Gaunt jnr who were Dartmouth's president and chairman respectively.

The following day one of Albion's all-time greats, full-back Jesse Pennington, celebrated his seventieth birthday.

On 25 August, the club's Annual General Meeting took place at The Hawthorns and chairman Major H. Wilson Keys announced a profit of £6,267 on the previous season, about £3,000 of which was the result of an approximate increase in attendance of 1,800 per match from 29,712 to 31,527. Major Keys, who had been a director of the club since 1930 and chairman since 1946, was made a life member of the club, an honour he referred to as 'the greatest anyone could hold'. Mr W.E. Jephcott, a director since 1941, did not seek re-election and was appointed vice-president. Mr W.W. Hackett CBE, the Rt Hon. John Dugdale PC MP and Sir Alexander Ramsay OBE were all re-elected as vice-presidents while Mr Len Pritchards joined the board of directors and thus teamed up with former player Mr T.W. Glidden, Mr W.H. Thursfield, Mr J.W. Gaunt jnr and Mr S.R. Shepherd JP. The Rt Hon. the Earl of Dartmouth GCVO TD DL was re-elected as Albion's president, while Mr Eph Smith retained the position as club secretary with Mr Alan Everiss his assistant.

Albion chairman Major H. Wilson Keys.

Albion: Heath; Rickaby, Millard; Dudley, Dugdale, Barlow; Griffin, Hodgkisson, Allen, Nicholls, Lee.

Bolton Wanderers: Hanson; Ball, Higgins; Wheeler, Barrass, Bell; Holden, Moir, Codd, Hassall, Parry.

UNITED BLITZED IN SECOND HALF

Date: Wednesday 26 August 1953
Location: Old Trafford
Attendance: 31,806

Match title: League
Referee: Mr P.F. Power (York)

Albion were unchanged for their midweek visit to Old Trafford, and for the first quarter of the game came under severe pressure as United's attack was playing flat out. But thanks to some dogged and at times confident defending, especially by Stan Rickaby, they conceded only one goal. That came in the twenty-first minute when Tommy Taylor, finding space, collected David Pegg's low cross to fire wide of Norman Heath.

Albion regrouped, counter-attacked quickly and within seven minutes grabbed an equaliser when Jimmy Dudley, playing in his 100th League game for the club, scored with a terrific shot from fully twenty-five yards, the ball striking both uprights before finding its way into the net. This goal seemed to inspire Albion's attack and for the remainder of the half they were far more threatening than United's.

Albion were also first out of the blocks at the start of the second period and Jack Crompton, the United goalkeeper, punched a thunderbolt from George Lee over the bar. At the other end Heath saved at the feet of Taylor.

The game was developing into a thrill-a-minute contest and continued pressure by the Albion attack earned its reward in the sixty-sixth minute when Johnny Nicholls, who had earlier missed two relatively easy chances, nipped in to beat Crompton as he left his line. Allen then had a shot deflected inches wide as Crompton scrambled across his line.

United, with nothing to lose, pushed men forward and twice Albion's goal had a narrow escape. But on seventy-three minutes left-winger Lee powered home a third goal to clinch victory and shoot the Baggies to the top of the table, ahead of Huddersfield Town on goal average. Wolves went down 3-2 at Sunderland and were now in sixteenth position, three points behind Albion. Early days though!

Club News

As Albion were winning at Old Trafford so the reserves were beating Manchester United 2-1 at The Hawthorns. Freddie Cox played his first game for the club and did well, as did Harry Haddington, who was making his home debut. But Stuart Williams took a nasty blow to his ankle. Almost 4,000 spectators saw the game.

Reg Ryan declared himself available for selection after being low with tonsillitis. Tim Rawlings received his call-up papers and was to join fellow players Reg Davies and Gerry Summers (both based in Germany), Barry Hatfield, Allan Crowshaw, Reg Cutler, Wilf Carter, Derek Kevan and Vic Willis in the forces.

Manchester United 1	Albion 3
Taylor	Dudley
	Nicholls
	Lee

Left: Jimmy Dudley gave Albion the lead with a brilliant 25-yard strike.

Below: Albion keeper Norman Heath and full-back Stan Rickaby cover a Tommy Taylor shot.

Manchester United: Crompton; Aston, Byrne; Gibson, Chilton, Cockburn; Berry, Rowley, Taylor, Lewis, Pegg.
Team: Heath; Rickaby, Millard; Dudley, Dugdale, Barlow; Griffin, Hodgkisson, Allen, Nicholls, Lee.

AT LAST, ALBION WIN AT DEEPDALE!

Date: Saturday 29 August 1953
Location: Deepdale
Attendance: 30,462

Match title: League
Referee: Mr W. Ratcliffe (Leek)

Albion, unchanged for the fourth game running, beat the 1952/53 League runners-up Preston North End in style to break a nineteen-year-old record of failing to win at Deepdale. In fact, their last victory on the ground had been 2-1, achieved back in December 1934.

Preston started strongly and England winger Tom Finney, after outwitting Len Millard, put his cross too near to keeper Norman Heath as Charlie Wayman moved in for the kill. Frank Griffin had to receive treatment for a kick on the right knee after just ten minutes and soon afterwards Ray Barlow deflected a crashing drive from Finney for a corner. Finney then fed Foster but Barlow and Millard closed in quickly to squash any danger. On thirty minutes George Lee, collecting Allen's shrewd pass, shot wide after rounding keeper George Thompson and then Jimmy Dudley was floored by a hefty challenge from Baxter.

Five minutes before the interval Albion took the lead. Millard scooped the ball down the left for Lee to chase. At speed, the winger delivered the perfect cross, left-footed, for Nicholls to head home from six yards: a great goal, one much appreciated by the crowd.

Early in the second half Thompson thwarted Nicholls and Griffin as Albion quickly got going. Preston responded and Wayman struck a post with a drive from fifteen yards, and Finney's low shot was turned aside by Heath. Len Millard then had a twenty-five-yarder saved at full length by Thompson, and Barlow's short backpass to Heath was intercepted by Wayman but Rickaby and Dugdale got back to cover the goal. Nicholls had a shot turned aside, and at the other end Millard hoofed the ball over his own crossbar after Heath had palmed out Wayman's shot. Two minutes from time Nicholls grabbed a second goal for Albion, turning in Ken Hodgkisson's cross from the right after some neat work by Griffin, who was having a fine match.

A good solid win for Albion, who dropped down a place, as Huddersfield took over at the top of the table. Wolves beat Cardiff City 3-1 at home to move up to tenth place, three points behind Albion. Two days later Stan Cullis' men won again, beating Sunderland 3-1 at Molineux to close within a point of the Baggies.

Club News

The *Albion News* pointed out that it was rare for Ronnie Allen to go five League games without scoring (one at the end of the previous season and four this term), but as the centre forward said: 'It doesn't matter who scores as long as they go into the opposition net.'

Preston North End 0

Albion 2
Nicholls (2)

Left: Two more goals for in-form Johnny Nicholls. *Centre:* Norman Heath made two excellent saves, one from Tom Finney. *Right:* Frank Griffin played well on Albion's right wing, as he did in the Cup Final!

Over 2,500 fans saw Albion reserves beat Stoke City reserves 5-0 in a Central League game at The Hawthorns on 29 August. Freddie Cox scored a hat-trick (including a penalty).

Joe Kennedy was injured in this game and straight away fears grew that he might require a cartilage operation, but it was only a groin strain.

Barry Hughes, aged sixteen, a Welsh schoolboy international, made his first appearance for Albion's third team in a 3-1 defeat by Bedworth Town on 31 August, the same day the reserves drew 1-1 with Manchester United reserves at Old Trafford.

Preston North End: Thompson; Cunningham, Scott; Mattinson, Marston, Dunn; Finney, Foster, Wayman, Baxter, Morrison.

Albion: Heath; Rickaby, Millard; Dudley, Dugdale, Barlow; Griffin, Hodgkisson, Allen, Nicholls, Lee.

17

FIRST DOUBLE OF THE SEASON

Date: Wednesday 2 September 1953   **Match title:** League
Location: The Hawthorns   **Referee:** Mr P.F. Power (York)
Attendance: 29,036

Unchanged Albion performed very well as they completed their first double of the season and at the same time recorded their fourth in the League over United (their last was in 1919/20). In front of a rather disappointing midweek crowd of just over 29,000, both teams started the game nervously. Albion had the first effort at goal but Johnny Nicholls sliced his shot wide. Tommy Taylor responded for United but generally there was very little to choose between the two teams during the first half's play. Then, after Frank Griffin's high looping centre had clipped the top of the United bar, Albion's right-back Stan Rickaby and his team-mate Jimmy Dudley collided with each other as they went to cut out a short pass delivered by Henry Cockburn and aimed for Jack Rowley. Both players required treatment; Dudley recovered but Rickaby was shaken and moved to centre forward. Ronnie Allen moved to inside right, Griffin and Ken Hodgkisson took over at right-back.

On thirty-five minutes, Rickaby, who had wandered out to the left wing, sent over a zipping cross which Griffin headed goalwards only to see Ray Wood, the United keeper, make a flying save. From the resulting corner, taken by Griffin, Wood fisted the ball back towards the flag. George Lee retrieved it and his low, crisp centre was smashed home by Allen, Roger Byrne attempting to clear the effort off the line with his head! Dennis Viollet, aged nineteen, who was making his first appearance of the season for United, almost equalised but his two close-range shots were smothered by Norman Heath, and then Rowley's low drive sped inches wide.

The game was fairly evenly matched throughout the second half. Wood saved magnificently from Hodgkisson, who had ventured forward, and Lee was only a foot off target with one of his left-footed rockets. At the other end of the field, Taylor (twice) and Viollet both had half-chances for United, Albion's skipper Len Millard clearing two of them with timely tackles as his defence coped quite well when danger threatened. With time running out, Albion scored a second goal. Allen centred from the right, the alert Nicholls crashed his shot goalwards but the ball struck United's full-back Johnny Aston on the line, rebounded against a post and dropped to the feet of Lee. The winger's drive bounced off another defender and with at least half a dozen players sprawled on the ground inside the penalty area, the ball shot up into the air where Hodgkisson found a gap to head it over the line.

Len Millard and Ray Barlow were the stars of Albion's defence, while Allen and Lee were on top of their game in attack. Jeff Whitefoot, Allenby Chilton, Aston and Johnny Berry were best for United.

Albion 2   **Manchester United 0**
   Allen
   Hodgkisson

United full-back Roger Byrne jumps in vain as Ronnie Allen's shot hits the back of the net.

As a result of this victory Albion moved two points clear of Huddersfield Town at the top of the Division One table. Wolves without a game dropped down to seventh.

Club News
Stan Rickaby underwent treatment on Thursday morning and declared himself fit to play against Spurs at the weekend. Reg Ryan also told his manager that he was now back to full fitness after his throat problems but goalkeeper Jimmy Sanders was still suffering some pain from his damaged wrist.

Albion: Heath; Rickaby, Millard; Dudley, Dugdale, Barlow; Griffin, Hodgkisson, Allen, Nicholls, Lee.
Manchester United: Wood; Aston, Byrne; Whitefoot, Chilton, Cockburn; Berry, Lewis, Taylor, Viollet, Rowley.

SPARKLING DISPLAY BY ALBION

Date: Saturday 5 September 1953　　**Match title:** League
Location: The Hawthorns　　**Referee:** Mr F. Cowen (Manchester)
Attendance: 43,168

Irish international Reg Ryan returned to Albion's forward line for the home game with Spurs, who had won four and lost one of their opening five matches – and they had moved menacingly into second place in the table after a 1-0 victory at Charlton forty-eight hours earlier. Albion took a grip of the game early on and after a couple of smart attacks aimed down both flanks, they swept into the lead on twelve minutes. Ray Barlow collected a loose ball in centre field and delivered a sizzling long pass to George Lee on the left. The winger raced to the byline before cutting the ball back into the heart of the Spurs penalty area. Two shots were charged down before the ball found its way back to Lee whose effort was blocked, only for the alert Ronnie Allen, following up, to find the back of the net from four yards.

Allen, Lee and Ryan all had shots at goal during the next twenty minutes while at the opposite end Len Duquemin was a lone forager for the Londoners, and he was getting very little change out of Jimmy Dugdale. Displaying stylish aggression, Albion continued to dominate the game. Ditchburn saved from Allen and Nicholls headed wide. Spurs weren't in it and all they could manage before half-time was a long-range effort from Eddie Baily, a toe-poke from Sonny Walters and a half-hit volley from Johnny Brooks, a £38,000 signing from Chelsea.

Early in the second half Brooks developed cramp and hobbled out to the wing. He had been there for barely two minutes when Albion scored again. In the forty-ninth minute Griffin got past left-back Willis and delivered a high cross. Nicholls, powering in, leapt head and shoulders above Harry Clarke and Bill Nicholson to nod the ball home for a fine goal. Just 120 seconds later it was 3-0 when Griffin, who was teasing Willis left, right and centre, sped past the Spurs full-back for the umpteenth time and his low cross was turned past his own keeper by the back-tracking Alf Ramsey. Only some superb saves from Ted Ditchburn, two cool clearances from Ramsey and some slogging work by Ronnie Burgess and Nicholson restricted Albion to three goals. It should have been more. Allen, Nicholls, Dudley and Ryan could have scored late on as Spurs wilted under pressure. Even when the Londoners did get in a shot, keeper Heath was there to save.

The *Sports Argus* reporter wrote: 'This sparkling Albion performance gets a diamond rating ... They were a team that touched the heights ... And one could see the influence of manager and former Spurs player Vic Buckingham at work: the quick short pass, the urgency of the defence men to use the ball, the work in the spaces and the variation in the crosses of wingers Lee and Griffin. The supporters this afternoon were exhilarated by

---

Albion 3　　　　　　　　　　　　　　　**Tottenham Hotspur 0**
　Allen
　Nicholls
　Ramsey (og)

a game rich in good football and gloriously coloured by a display of the finer arts, craft and intelligence. They saw Albion sweep to a dominating victory.' The *Daily Express* correspondent stated that 'Jimmy Dugdale, fast, sure-footed, gave Duquemin little rope...Ronnie Allen is surely the best centre forward in football...Reg Ryan was almost as big a threat...Griffin could give any defender yards from a level start and still got to the ball first...Jimmy Dudley showed some great attacking play and Ray Barlow guided and prompted his forwards with a flow of text-book passes. Heath was impressive in goal, too.'

This emphatic victory made it five wins out of six for Albion whose goal tally was thirteen for and only two against. They had ten points, three more than Blackpool, Burnley and Wolves, who moved into fourth spot after a 3-2 win at Arsenal.

Club News

Two players were receiving treatment for broken noses: Sid Dunn and Joe Kennedy, who was still struggling with his groin. Stuart Williams (ankle) was also receiving treatment, likewise Ken Hodgkisson (split eye) while goalkeeper Jimmy Sanders was told he could recommence full training. Vic Willis was posted to the Middle East to continue his National Service.

Jimmy Dugdale, fast and sure-footed.

Albion: Heath; Rickaby, Millard; Dudley, Dugdale, Barlow; Griffin, Ryan, Allen, Nicholls, Lee.

Tottenham Hotspur: Ditchburn; Ramsey, Withers; Nicholson, Clarke, Burgess; Walters, Brooks, Duquemin, Baily, Robb.

A MATCH TO ENTHUSE OVER

Date: Wednesday 9 September 1953
Location: The Hawthorns
Attendance: 32,953

Match title: League
Referee: Mr T. Seymour (Wakefield)

Vic Buckingham named an unchanged side for this encounter with Newcastle United, Albion's third home League game in succession. The Geordies had won two and drawn two of their opening five matches and had already scored eleven goals – so an attack-minded ninety minutes was assured!

It was a match to enthuse over as the twenty-two players painted an exciting, brightly hued canvas. The crowd roared constantly with the thrill of an all-action contest and at the end stood and cheered both teams off the pitch after a great battle.

Roy Peskett, covering the match for the *Daily Mail*, wrote: 'Twice Albion were behind, the second time for just a minute after they had classically carved out an equaliser – against a great Newcastle defence enough to deter the stoutest of hearts. But Albion kept their heads, if not their places. Their forwards were like five blobs of quicksilver as they raced hither too and yon to baffle Brennan and his men.'

Although the first half was goalless, both keepers were kept busy. Jackie Milburn, playing forcibly on the Newcastle right, was a constant danger and twice brought Norman Heath to his knees with stinging drives. Centre forward Vic Keeble and left-winger Bobby Mitchell also had efforts blocked by Heath while George Hannah's free-kick was only inches wide. For Albion, Allen, Nicholls (twice) and Reg Ryan all drove in shots which Ronnie Simpson dealt with comfortably, although he was forced to make flying saves from Lee and, early in the second half, from Allen. The ball sped back and forth across the field as in a tennis rally before Allen fired in a splendid cross from the right which Lee, moving inside full-back Bobby Cowell, rose to head powerfully towards goal, only to see the agile Simpson, at full stretch, dive to flick it round his right-hand post.

On fifty-two minutes Newcastle edged in front, perhaps slightly against the run of play. Mitchell, eluding Stan Rickaby near the halfway line, cut inside and wove his way through the middle, and when everybody expected him to pass to Reg Davies, racing up alongside, he drove the ball sweetly past Heath from twenty-five yards. Albion defended stubbornly for a time and then counter-attacked, only for Nicholls to miss the target by inches following a timely pass from Allen.

With twenty-five minutes remaining Reg Ryan powered in the equaliser at the Smethwick End. A move involving five players, with Barlow at the centre, sliced open the Newcastle defence and Ryan, moving across the edge of the area from right to left, struck his shot past Simpson with great precision and timing. Almost immediately the visitors raced down the other end of the field and regained the lead. Milburn, who had a fine

---

Albion 2
Ryan
Barlow

Newcastle United 2
Mitchell
Keeble

An enthusiastic crowd at The Hawthorns.

game, burst into the penalty area and fired in a shot that bounced off Dugdale straight into the path of Keeble who made no mistake from eight yards. Fifteen minutes from time Mitchell was robbed of a goal by an amazing goal line clearance from Dugdale. The winger dribbled into the area and beat Heath only for the Albion centre half to head the ball to safety in amazing fashion. If that had gone in, Albion would have lost the match, but with masterful wing half Ray Barlow driving forward, a second equaliser arrived nine minutes from time. Griffin, on receiving a short pass from Jimmy Dudley, set off down the right wing. His head-high cross came flying over and as it dropped, Barlow, who had made ground rapidly, flew through the air to head the ball hard and low into the farthest corner of the net from eighteen yards. It was a cracking goal that earned Albion a point.

Wolves, who had beaten Liverpool 2-1 two days earlier, were now in third spot, with Burnley in second, both teams on 10 points, two behind Albion.

Club News

While Albion's first XI were battling it out with Newcastle at The Hawthorns, the reserves were involved in a ten-goal thriller at Preston, which they won 6-4 with Elfed Evans scoring five times. Wilf Carter netted the other as he went through the home defence like 'Neville Duke at his fastest' to belt the ball home.

Club trainer Arthur Fitton entered hospital for a minor operation to remove a small piece of bone lodged in his throat and Elfed Evans went down with tonsillitis.

Albion: Heath; Rickaby, Millard; Dudley, Dugdale, Barlow; Griffin, Ryan, Allen, Nicholls, Lee.

Newcastle United: Simpson; Cowell, Batty; Stokoe, Brennan, Crowe; Milburn, Davies, Keeble, Hannah, Mitchell.

ALBION PRODUCE 'MOOR' OF THE SAME

Date: Saturday 12 September 1953
Location: Turf Moor
Attendance: 38,948

Match title: League
Referee: Mr F.L. Overton (Derby)

Fielding the same eleven players who had fought to salvage a point at home to Newcastle, Albion travelled to Turf Moor for their eighth League game of the season. It had not been a lucky ground for the Baggies who had succumbed to 6-1 and 5-0 defeats on their two previous visits, but this time they produced a fine performance and ran out 4-1 winners.

The usually well-organised and mean Burnley defence was torn to ribbons by a quick-moving, quick-thinking Albion attack. Vic Buckingham's men produced perhaps their best display of the season so far and if it hadn't been for the Burnley keeper, their tally might have been doubled. The outstanding feature of the game was the magnificent display of the three half-backs, Dudley, Dugdale and Barlow. The trio were responsible for shattering the hopes of the Burnley forwards who never really threatened after left-winger Pilkington had received an early injury. Throughout the game Barlow was a conspicuous figure and Stan Rickaby, too, gave an exhilarating display at right-back.

The Burnley defence was not too impressive under pressure and was continually forced back, conceding a dozen or so free-kicks in dangerous positions, giving Ronnie Allen a right old buffeting. The scoring commenced in the eighteenth minute when Frank Griffin fired over a teasing cross from the right. Burnley full-back Jock Aird attempted to steer it back to his keeper, but only succeeded in teeing up Allen, who scored with ease from eight yards. After Allen, Griffin and Dudley had all gone close, Albion increased their lead on thirty-four minutes when Griffin once more got the better of Doug Winton down the right and his cross was headed powerfully home by Johnny Nicholls.

Either side of half-time Burnley had their best period, but it was against the run of play when on sixty-four minutes they reduced the deficit through Roy Stephenson, who beat Heath with an angled drive after some neat work down the right by Billy Gray. Albion responded with a series of attacks aimed down the Burnley right, and from one of them, George Lee made goal number three in the seventy-seventh minute, Nicholls gleefully guiding home his astute cross from the left. Five minutes from time Reg Ryan, eluding Jimmy Adamson's challenge, completed the scoring to put on the icing on top of an impressive victory for Albion. Twice in the last two minutes Thompson pulled off fine saves from Allen and Nicholls, and Griffin fired into the side netting when well placed.

Dugdale completely blocked out the threat of the England 'B' international, centre forward Bill Holden, and was praised for his excellent display by his manager after the game. Albion were still on top of the ladder with fourteen points, but Wolves, after beating Portsmouth 4-3 at Molineux, leap-frogged over Burnley into second place.

Burnley 1	**Albion 4**
Stephenson	Allen
	Nicholls (2)
	Ryan

Club News

It was revealed that the Scotland selectors had been at Turf Moor to watch Albion's wing half Jimmy Dudley.

Following their exciting 6-4 win at Preston, Albion's Second XI beat Newcastle United reserves 5-0 at St James' Park on 9 September. Forwards Wilf Carter, Brian Whitehouse and Dave Mountford and wing halves Billy Brookes and Stuart Williams scored the goals. Joe Kennedy and Jimmy Sanders both returned to action.

Ronnie Allen, in good form, was ready to appear in his 150th first team game for Albion in the return fixture with Newcastle. He made his debut for the club against Wolves in March 1950.

Derek Kevan returned to The Hawthorns after scoring six times for his battalion team.

Left-winger George Lee made Albion's second goal for Johnny Nicholls.

Burnley: Thompson; Aird, Winton; Adamson, Cummings, Attwell; Gray, McIlroy, Holden, Stephenson, Pilkington.

Albion: Heath; Rickaby, Millard; Dudley, Dugdale, Barlow; Griffin, Ryan, Allen, Nicholls, Lee.

THE MAGNIFICENT SEVEN

Date: Wednesday 16 September 1953   **Match title:** League
Location: St James' Park   **Referee:** Mr T. Seymour (Wakefield)
Attendance: 58,075

In-form and unchanged Albion reached the pinnacle of football perfection with this magnificent victory at St James' Park. Not that Newcastle played badly. Albion played better, created more chances and in the end they ran out convincing winners. Forty-five years earlier, in 1908, Newcastle had been beaten 9-1 at home by Sunderland. Albion came close emulating that scoreline – and if it hadn't been for keeper Ronnie Simpson, they would have certainly reached double figures.

It was certainly an impressive performance and the newspapers were full of it! 'Wonderful West Brom Score 7', 'The Magnificent 7', 'Albion's Jamboree At Newcastle', 'Albion Goal Rush' 'Tyneside Faithful Dazed' and 'Red For Danger' (for the coloured shirts the Albion players wore) were a few of the headlines describing this victory.

Johnny Nicholls celebrated his fiftieth senior appearance with his first hat-trick for the club and his presence in and around the penalty area gave the home defence palpitations. Ronnie Allen had an early chance (following a slip by Frank Brennan) but his shot was too close to keeper Simpson and Bobby Cowell dashed back to clear the loose ball as Nicholls raced in. Soon afterwards Allen headed home only for the linesman's flag to rule offside, and in quick succession Frank Griffin, Allen and Nicholls all had chances. Newcastle's best effort came from Jackie Milburn, but that went well wide.

Amazingly it was thirty-three minutes before the first goal arrived. Smart passing between Ray Barlow and Jimmy Dudley, with a touch from Reg Ryan, sent Allen racing forward and his eighteen-yard drive flew past Simpson like a rocket. Two minutes later a powerful header from Allen was pushed against the crossbar by Simpson, only for the alert Nicholls to charge forward to nod in the rebound. 2-0. Both goalkeepers were then brought into action before Albion took a 3-0 lead on forty-two minutes. Allen found space to get in a low ground shot. The ball struck Frank Brennan and sent keeper Simpson the wrong way, before crossing the line with Cowell chasing back in a vain attempt to clear.

Urged on by the loyal supporters in the 58,000-plus crowd, Newcastle surged forward at the start of the second-half and reduced the deficit on forty-six minutes when Vic Keeble netted after some good work by Milburn and George Hannah. Albion were made to defend resolutely as the Magpies pressed forward, and on the hour mark Milburn was again in the thick of the action as Bobby Mitchell pounced to make it 3-2. Game on, but Albion quickly responded and within five minutes Nicholls was on hand to make it 4-2, side-footing home as Cowell failed to cut out Lee's pass. Back came United and Mitchell, finding space, made it 4-3 with fifteen minutes remaining. At this juncture one felt that

Newcastle United 3
    Keeble
    Mitchell (2)

Albion 7
    Nicholls (3)
    Allen (2)
    Griffin, Ryan

Johnny Nicholls taps home
the first of his three goals.

Albion might shut up shop. No way. They stormed forward and scored three more goals in rapid succession, first through Nicholls, completing his hat-trick, then via Paddy Ryan's left foot and finally from Griffin, whose effort was described as 'an elegant finish'. Right on full time Simpson prevented Allen from completing his hat-trick with a great save.

This was truly a great win for the Baggies, their best on the road in Division One since their 7-0 mauling of Aston Villa in 1935. And it was the first time Newcastle had conceded seven goals at home since November 1939 (when they were beaten 7-4 by Portsmouth). This victory made it sixteen goals in three visits to St James' Park for rampant Albion, who had won 4-1 and 5-3 on that ground in their two previous visits. During the day the funeral took place of the Newcastle United director Lord Westwood, and both sets of players wore black armbands during the game.

With nine fixtures completed, Albion had gained a three-point lead over Wolves (16-13) after the Molineux side drew 1-1 at Liverpool. Huddersfield and Burnley were third and fourth.

Club News

The Albion party travelled to Whitley Bay the day before the Newcastle game, and after beating the Magpies so emphatically they returned to the seaside resort before travelling down to the Midlands on the Thursday afternoon.

Three trialists played in the Colts team that beat Darlaston 3-1 on 12 September.

Gerry Summers was informed that he would be demobbed inside four months ('Watch out Ray Barlow' stated the *Albion News*).

Manager Vic Buckingham appeared on a TV programme shown 'live' from Lichfield.

Newcastle United: Simpson; Cowell, Batty; Scoular, Brennan, Crowe; Milburn, Davies, Keeble, Hannah, Mitchell.

Albion: Heath; Rickaby, Millard; Dudley, Dugdale, Barlow; Griffin, Ryan, Allen, Nicholls, Lee.

DISAPPOINTING DEFEAT

Date: Saturday 19 September 1953
Location: The Hawthorns
Attendance: 43,809

Match title: League
Referee: Mr R.E. Tarratt (Horsham)

Unchanged for the fifth successive game and on an unbeaten run of twelve League games, Albion went into their clash with twelfth-placed Charlton full of confidence, especially after that terrific result on Tyneside. Indeed, they were strongly fancied to beat the Londoners, who had won four and lost four of their opening eight matches. But as so often happens in football – and, indeed, in horse racing – the favourites don't always win!

The Addicks, strong in defence and fast and direct in their forward play, matched Albion kick for kick and in the end perhaps deserved to win for their plucky resistance. Baggies boss Vic Buckingham wasn't too happy with his team's performance, strongly criticising his defence for 'a lack of concentration'. Alan Neale, reporting in the *Sports Argus*, said: 'Albion did rather too much fiddling about, the attack often lacking rhythm.' In the end Charlton had to thank their veteran goalkeeper Sam Bartram for this victory. He played superbly, and late on pulled off two terrific saves to deny Jimmy Dudley and Ronnie Allen from grabbing a third equaliser.

After some tedious early play, Charlton shot in front on eight minutes when John Evans, unmarked, collected Billy Kiernan's left-wing cross and planted a low shot past Norman Heath from fifteen yards. Following two near misses, one at either end, Ray Barlow equalised on eighteen minutes. Standing unmarked on the edge of the penalty area, he suddenly saw an opening and let fly with a thumping 25-yarder which flew hard and low past Bartram. However, some slack marking at the back allowed the visitors to reclaim their lead three minutes later, and again Evans was the marksman, scoring from distance after being given a free sight at goal, his 25-yard effort flying past the unsighted Heath. Twice Albion came close to levelling things up before half-time, but they could also have found themselves 1-3 down when Stuart Leary shot wide from just inside the box.

Three minutes into the second half Albion netted their second equaliser, Frank Griffin scoring from twelve yards after Barlow and Nicholls had found a way through down the right. It was the latter who supplied the final pass for the winger to fire home. Heath saved at the feet of Leary as Charlton came again and it was no surprise when, on sixty-five minutes, the South African Leary scored what was to prove the winning goal. A measured crossfield ball found right-winger Gordon Hurst, and from his centre Leary got between Dudley and Dugdale to beat Heath with a first-time shot. Bartram then saved magnificently from Barlow at the expense of a corner, and from Griffin's inswinging flag-kick Fenton cleared the ball off the line. Shortly afterwards, Bartram denied Dudley, and both Allen and Nicholls screwed shots wide. Late in the game Millard hobbled off with

Albion 2
Barlow
Griffin

Charlton Athletic 3
Evans (2)
Leary

Sam Bartram dives but fails to stop Frank Griffin's twelve-yard shot from entering the net.

an ankle injury, going straight to hospital. This was Charlton's first League win at The Hawthorns since 1937. By drawing 0-0 at Blackpool, Wolves closed the gap on Albion at the top of Division One to two points (16-14) although Huddersfield Town (also on fourteen points) were placed second on goal average.

Club News

Two England selectors, chairman Harold Shentall and David Wiseman, were at The Hawthorns watching Albion's game with Charlton.

Skipper Len Millard had an X-ray on his damaged ankle. Thankfully the doctors diagnosed no serious problem but stressed that he would certainly miss the next game.

Ray Barlow travelled as a reserve with the Football League side that took on the Irish League in Belfast on Wednesday 23 September.

After beating Newcastle United 3-0, Albion's reserves drew 0-0 with Chesterfield to move into fourth position in the Central League.

Two Albion players – right-back Don Howe and outside right Grenville Jones – were selected to represent the Birmingham County FA against the South African tourists at Moor Green on 26 September.

Albion: Heath; Rickaby, Millard; Dudley, Dugdale, Barlow; Griffin, Ryan, Allen, Nicholls, Lee.

Charlton Athletic: Bartram; Campbell, Ellis; Fenton, Ufton, Hammond; Hurst, O'Linn, Leary, Evans, Kiernan.

OWLS' NEST FEATHERED BY THE THROSTLES

Date: Saturday 26 September 1953
Location: Hillsborough
Attendance: 45,503

Match title: League
Referee: Mr A. Bond (London)

Stuart Williams was introduced at left-back in place of the injured Len Millard for Albion's trip to Hillsborough, this being the first change made by manager Vic Buckingham in five matches. On a bright, sunny afternoon, the Baggies, wearing red shorts and white shirts, failed to produce the sparkle they were capable of but still did enough to record their fifth successive away win and brush aside the previous week's defeat at the hands of Charlton Athletic. There were far too many heart-fluttering moments during the course of the last thirty minutes before they finally registered two more points, and manager Buckingham admitted afterwards that 'it was not a good performance, a gritty one yes.'

Albion certainly played some excellent football during the first half and in fact they should have gone in at the break in an unassailable position. Time and again during the first half they split open the Wednesday defence with some delightful passing, and created enough chances to have scored at least six goals. They managed only one – and that flew into the net on seventeen minutes off the leg of home Scottish-born defender Jim McAnearney, although Frank Griffin, who fired in the shot, later claimed the goal. Reg Ryan, clean through, shot straight at Owls keeper Ryalls, and then Nicholls fired wide from a good position. Soon afterwards, with Albion in complete control, the same player headed Allen's cross goalwards, turned to celebrate scoring, only to find the ball had bounced clear off an upright. If he'd watched what was happening, he would surely have had a very simple tap-in! Two minutes later Ryan's piledriver stung the fingers of Brian Ryalls before fizzing upwards and hitting the crossbar. Right on half-time Griffin fired into the side-netting after racing onto a shrewd pass from Nicholls.

Nicholls unfortunately took a nasty knock on his ankle during the first half and returned after the break with heavy strapping over his boot. He battled on, however, and doubled Albion's score with a smart back-header from Barlow's delicate lob on forty-nine minutes. Wednesday responded, and after Albert Quixall had gone down on the edge of the area following a double challenge by Barlow and Dugdale, an almighty scramble ensued before Heath dropped on the ball.

Pushing more men forward, Wednesday got a goal back on sixty-seven minutes when Jackie Sewell, later to win an FA Cup winner's medal with Aston Villa, found the net from just inside the penalty area after the inside forward had charged down Stan Rickaby's attempted clearance. Growing in confidence, the Owls attacked with more adventure and deservedly drew level on seventy-three minutes through left-winger Dennis Woodhead. He collected a short pass from Sewell, cut inside and dummied Rickaby before bending

Sheffield Wednesday 2	Albion 3
Sewell	Griffin
Woodhead	Nicholls
	Lee

Far left: Ray Barlow skippered Albion in the absence of Len Millard. *Left:* Stuart Williams did well in the left-back position.

a magnificent shot past Heath from the edge of the penalty area. A fine goal. This in no way upset Albion who went straight down to the other end and paid Wednesday back. Griffin weaved his way through, found space and crossed perfectly for George 'Ada' Lee to stoop low and head home what was to be the winning goal. Wednesday fought to the last but Albion's bold and determined defenders held firm, and although a trifle more busy than one would have wished, remained calm and another victory was safely secured.

Back in the Midlands, Wolves walloped Chelsea 8-1 to keep within striking distance of Albion at the top of the table. They had sixteen points, the same number as second-placed Huddersfield, while Albion were on eighteen.

Club News

Again two England selectors watched Albion's match at Hillsborough, with Ray Barlow and Ronnie Allen under close scrutiny.

Jimmy Dudley was named in the Scotland 'shadow eleven' during the week (meaning that if the first-choice player drops out then his replacement automatically steps forward).

A crowd of 2,340 saw Albion lose their home Central League game against Sheffield Wednesday 2-1 on 26 September.

Albion's Dave Mountford joined team-mates Don Howe and Grenville Jones in the Birmingham County FA side that drew with the South Africans at Moor Green.

Dick Jones, a winger from Llanrwst Town, signed professional forms for Albion on 28 September for a month's trial.

Two youngsters, Kenneth Clarke and John West, both scored hat-tricks as Albion's junior side beat Kryle Hall 9-0 in a Birmingham Youth Committee League game at the end of September.

Sheffield Wednesday: Ryalls; Conway, Curtis; McAnearney, O'Donnell, Gannon; Finney, Quixall, Jordan, Sewell, Woodhead.

Albion: Heath; Rickaby, S. Williams; Dudley, Dugdale, Barlow; Griffin, Ryan, Allen, Nicholls, Lee.

POOR DISPLAY, BUT TWO MORE POINTS

Date: Saturday 3 October 1953
Location: The Hawthorns
Attendance: 37,042

Match title: League
Referee: Mr G. Gibson (Manchester)

A fit-again Len Millard returned to the side to face Middlesbrough but there was no Reg Ryan. He was given permission to play for the Republic of Ireland against France in Dublin the following day (Sunday). His place was taken by winger Freddie Cox, who therefore made his senior debut for the Baggies, albeit at inside-right. England star Wilf Mannion was in the Boro side and he was by far the best player on view in a rather disappointing and in truth poor game. In fact only the gramophone, for broadcasting at half-time and full time, played well!

Cox struggled to get into the game early on, as did both Albion wingers, Frank Griffin and George Lee. However, Boro's two wingers, Joe Rayment and Geoff Walker, had early chances to show their worth. Up to six passes in succession often went hopelessly astray as both sides struggled to get going on a bumpy pitch. Jimmy Dudley put in Albion's first shot (wide) while Lindy Delaphena was off target for Boro. On nineteen minutes Johnny Nicholls popped up six yards out to give Albion the lead. Cox, taking a free-kick quickly, combined with Griffin in a smart one-two down the right, and when the ball eventually found its way across the face of the goal, bypassing keeper Rolando Ugolini and the grounded Ray Bilcliff, Nicholls was there waiting for an easy goal. After some sluggish play Boro drew level on thirty-five minutes when the unmarked Johnny Spuhler scored from close range after hesitancy in the home defence – thus gaining a little tangible reward for some enterprising play which preceded the goal.

It was not until the fiftieth minute that Albion broke through again, squeezing through the tight wire mesh of some midfield closeness. A well-struck Allen pass found Griffin out on the right. He delivered a first-time cross to the far side of the Boro penalty area where his fellow winger George Lee, unmarked, crashed the ball home from six yards.

Although Wilf Mannion, who found Jimmy Dudley a difficult opponent throughout, tried his best to inject some life into the midfield exchanges, the game itself drifted into stagnation as the minutes ticked by, and there were only two worthwhile efforts fired in on goal during the last quarter of an hour. Rayment hooked in a beauty from five yards for Boro which hit Heath and rebounded to safety, while at the other end Allen sent a twenty-yard drive well wide and Dudley almost got on the end of a right-wing cross.

Two more points in the bag but it was a game best forgotten. Wolves drew 3-3 away at Sheffield United, and as a result slipped three points behind Albion (20-17) at the top end of the League table. Huddersfield Town, Albion's next opponents, were second on eighteen with Charlton Athletic fourth on sixteen.

Albion 2
Nicholls
Lee

Middlesbrough 1
Spuhler

Club News

Reg Ryan missed a penalty, but tucked away the rebound, as the Republic of Ireland lost 5-3 to France in Dublin.

Ray Barlow was named as a reserve for England for the Home International match against Wales at Cardiff on 10 October. And Jimmy Dugdale received notice that he would play centre half for the FA XI against the RAF on 14 October. Joe Kennedy played in this same fixture the previous season.

Four Albion players – Jim Garbett, Barry Hughes, Barry Cooke and Stan Purvis – all represented the Birmingham County FA at Hereford on 3 October.

Jimmy Dudley almost gets to a
low cross from Frank Griffin.

Albion: Heath; Rickaby, Millard; Dudley, Dugdale, Barlow; Griffin, Cox, Allen, Nicholls, Lee.

Middlesbrough: Ugolini; Bilcliff, Hepple; Bell, Robinson, Gordon; Rayment, Delaphena, Spuhler, Mannion, Walker.

ALLEN SUPERB, ALBION STIFLE TERRIERS' BARK

Date: Saturday 10 October 1953
Location: The Hawthorns
Attendance: 47,043

Match title: League
Referee: Mr J. Houston (Lytham St Anne's)

With Ray Barlow on duty with England in Cardiff, Billy Brookes was given his first taste of competitive League football against Huddersfield Town. And he played well as The Hawthorns' faithful were treated to a display of brilliant attacking football by the Baggies. A useful Huddersfield side, lively enough at the start of each half, had to endure wave after wave of fierce Albion pressure, and in the end were lucky not to concede more goals. At times Albion were brilliant. Their superiority came from the inspiration provided by Ronnie Allen who netted a wonderful hat-trick, his partner Johnny Nicholls scoring the other, Generally the whole team played exceedingly well on an afternoon when the Yorkshire Terriers lost their bite completely!

The game had been in progress for just eleven minutes when Allen, lingering just inside the penalty area, nodded Stan Rickaby's lob onto Reg Ryan. Allen held back, took the return pass and cracked home a right-foot volley from fully thirty yards, the ball never rising above six inches off the ground before burying itself in the net. Frank Griffin fired inches wide and Allen's dipping half-volley dropped just over the bar as Huddersfield came under more pressure.

On the half-hour mark Nicholls made it 2-0. Jimmy Dudley fed Allen who quickly switched the line of play and sent his 'twin goalpoacher' streaking through the middle. Nicholls finished with a powerful right-footed shot from eighteen yards, keeper Harry Mills standing no chance whatsoever of saving. Before half-time Allen had a smart header saved on the line and George Lee's low cross evaded everybody as it flew across the face of the goal and out for a throw-in near the corner flag on the opposite side of the pitch. Huddersfield's only worthwhile efforts during the first half came from Willie Davie and Ray Glazzard, neither of which troubled Norman Heath.

Glazzard had a chance early in the second half, but was off-target, and after that it was all Albion, except for the odd Huddersfield counter-attack. Allen lobbed over Ron Staniforth and keeper Mills but saw the ball bounce clear off an upright. Nicholls then fired straight at the keeper and another Allen effort went inches wide. Both Alistair Gunn and Glazzard had openings for the visitors but Heath denied both of them with smothering saves, while Dudley stopped Vic Metcalf in his tracks with a blocked tackle and then Davie scooped an effort over the bar. Despite Huddersfield's occasional flourishes, Albion had most of the play and they creating several chances, but had to wait until the last ten minutes before adding to their goal tally. On eighty-one minutes the supreme artistry of Allen was again in evidence when he worked in from the right edge

---

Albion 4
Allen (3)
Nicholls

Huddersfield Town 0

Far left: Billy Brookes made a sound debut.

Left: Brian Whitehouse, awaiting a call from the Army!

of the penalty area and with utmost coolness lofted the ball sweetly over the Mills' head into the far corner of the net. Four minutes later – after Heath had saved from Glazzard – Allen raced into the box, got between Bill McGarry and Don McEvoy to crack Lee's low centre high into the net.

Albion's biggest crowd of the season (at the time) went home delighted after seeing a fine display of attacking football from Buckingham's team. Albion were now three points clear of Wolves (2-1 winners at Newcastle) at the top of the table.

Club News

Allen's hat-trick against Huddersfield was his third for Albion, following his feats against Bolton (1951) and Wolves (1952).

Johnny Nicholls' 14th goal of the season (*v.* Huddersfield) took him to the top of the Division One scoring charts.

Jimmy Dugdale received his first representative honour when he played for the Football Association against the RAF at White Hart Lane on 14 October.

Almost 4,000 spectators saw Albion's second string lose 3-1 at Everton, Allan Crowshaw netting a beauty for the Baggies.

Reg Ryan was informed that he had been selected for the Republic of Ireland side to play Luxembourg in Dublin on 28 October.

Albion: Heath; Rickaby, Millard; Dudley, Dugdale, Brookes; Griffin, Ryan, Allen, Nicholls, Lee.

Huddersfield Town: Mills; Staniforth, Howe; McGarry, McEvoy, Quested; Gunn, Watson, Glazzard, Davie, Metcalf.

ALBION BLUNT THE YORKSHIRE BLADES

Date: Saturday 17 October 1953
Location: Bramall Lane
Attendance: 35,114

Match title: League
Referee: Mr H. Haworth (Blackburn)

Albion were at full strength for their visit to Bramall Lane, where they succeeded in keeping up their amazing away form with their seventh successive victory on the road, including one at the tail-end of the previous campaign. Sheffield United, newly promoted along with Huddersfield Town, were lying sixth from bottom with only ten points, but on the day they played much better than Albion as Vic Buckingham's side chose to produce their worst away performance of the season so far – yet they still managed to win!

Albion won two corners in the first two minutes, both proving fruitless. Jimmy Hagan, later to become manager at The Hawthorns (1963-67) set up the first chance for Harold Brook, but his effort was well saved by the diving Norman Heath in the Albion goal. In the eighth minute Albion took the lead when home keeper Ted Burgin could only parry Reg Ryan's low cross-shot (some reports say he fumbled the ball). Whatever happened, Ronnie Allen was on hand to tap it over the line from no more than four yards. Soon afterwards Allen sent in a cracking 25-yard drive past Burgin's post and the same player practically floored Blades centre half Howard Johnson with another rasping drive. Albion again won two quickfire corners (gained by the impressive Frank Griffin), while at the other end Stan Rickaby had to be alert to thwart a dangerous run by Derek Hawksworth. United continued to attack and Hagan, Hawksworth (again) and Brook all had half-chances, while wing half Colin Rawson fired high and wide from well outside the penalty area.

On the resumption, Ryan overran Allen's pass when well-placed, before the Baggies had an escape on fifty minutes when Alf Bottom shot straight at Heath from six yards. United appealed, in vain, for a penalty after Jimmy Dugdale had handled, but the free-kick was awarded outside the area. On sixty-five minutes United drew level. For once Hagan, with some clever footwork, outwitted both Ray Barlow and Len Millard on the left-hand side of the field, before delivering a deft pass into the middle where the unmarked Alf Ringstead was waiting to steer the ball past Heath from ten yards. United, looking rather anxious at times but still holding the ball well, went for more but a resilient Albion defence stood firm. After Johnson had been spoken to by referee Haworth for a crude and reckless challenge on Griffin, Heath was immediately forced into action as he fisted away a dangerous cross from Hagan.

With only five minutes remaining, Albion, perhaps surprisingly, grabbed the winner. Griffin, who was perhaps the best player on the field, skipped past Graham Shaw before slipping a pass inside to Allen who, in turn, fed Nicholls whose low shot beat Burgin all ends up. There was a late flourish by United but Albion held on – just – and duly secured

---

Sheffield United 1
Ringstead

Albion 2
Allen
Nicholls

another victory. Wolves beat Manchester United 3-1 at Molineux, so it was as you were at the top: Albion 24 points, Wolves 21, Huddersfield Town 20.

Club News

Ray Barlow was once again named as reserve by England for the international match *v.* Rest of Europe (FIFA) at Wembley on 21 October. Ronnie Allen accompanied him on the bench to watch the 4-4 draw.

On 23 October, utility forward Dave Mountford was transferred back to Crewe Alexandra for £33,000. He made five appearances for Albion, whom he joined in December 1951 from Gresty Road.

Despite Freddie Cox's penalty, Albion's Second XI lost 2-1 at home to Wolves.

Four Albion players were named in the Birmingham County FA side for the FA County youth match on 24 October.

Albion's youngsters started their FA Youth Cup campaign with a 1-0 away win in the second round at Chesterfield, Brian Whitehouse's penalty proving decisive. Skipper Don Howe was magnificent at right-back.

Albion's keeper Norman Heath gathers a cross during the first half of Albion's win at Bramall Lane. Ray Barlow (6) and Jimmy Dugdale (centre) are the other Albion players in the picture.

Sheffield United: Burgin; Furniss, G. Shaw; J. Shaw, Johnson, Rawson; Ringstead, Hagan, Bottom, Brook, Hawksworth.

Albion: Heath; Rickaby, Millard; Dudley, Dugdale, Barlow; Griffin, Ryan, Allen, Nicholls, Lee.

HOTSHOT ALLEN THE HERO AGAIN!

Date: Saturday 24 October 1953
Location: The Hawthorns
Attendance: 35,443

Match title: League
Referee: Mr R. P. Hartley (Burnley)

This seven-goal thriller at The Hawthorns was staged in three chapters, with Albion the heroes at the finish. Albion dominated the first chapter, Chelsea the second and the Baggies the third.

Albion, unchanged after Frank Griffin passed a fitness test, went 2-0 up in the first twelve minutes, Ronnie Allen claiming both goals just 120 seconds apart. This was after Johnny Nicholls had somehow scooped the ball over the bar early on. His first, in the tenth minute, came from Griffin's right-wing corner. The Albion centre forward, leaving his marker, raced across the goal to meet the winger's flag-kick right-footed, to leave keeper Bill Robertson helpless with a tremendous volley. Two minutes later, Allen, in space, turned quickly to beat Robertson with a snap-shot after Lee's cross from the left had caused panic in the Chelsea ranks, three defenders all failing to clear the danger. But shocks were in store for the home supporters who had settled down in expectation of seeing some real fireworks from the Baggies!

Chelsea, although stunned, bounced back quickly. Overshadowing the League leaders with some enterprising forward play, they got back on level terms, Roy Bentley claiming both goals after lapses in the Albion defence. The England international made it 2-1 in the seventeenth minute when he was left with a free shot at goal after keeper Norman Heath, under pressure it must be said, had missed with an attempted punch at tricky nineteen-year-old Frank Blunstone's left-wing cross. After two near misses at the Albion end of the field, Bentley levelled things up on thirty-eight minutes. Right-winger Eric Parsons, squeezing past Len Millard, cut the ball back for the centre forward to slam a right-foot shot towards the goal from the edge of the box. Stan Rickaby tried in vain to keep the ball from crossing the line. There were goalmouth thrills aplenty after that; Heath saved from Parsons, Ray Barlow kicked a Chelsea effort off the line, George Lee hit the bar at the other end and Allen fired over. Chelsea were denied a penalty when Johnnie McNichol was brought down, and Bentley headed wide. Frantic stuff.

Eight minutes after the interval Allen completed his hat-trick with another stunning shot. Griffin's corner was played short for Allen, whose first effort was blocked by McNichol. Ryan collected the loose ball, and his strike was also charged down. Allen, watching and waiting, pounced, and the England man did the rest in clinical fashion, cracking the ball high into the net on the half-volley from twelve yards. Almost immediately McNichol was denied an equaliser by the width of the crossbar, and soon afterwards his colleague Les Stubbs headed against the bar. Albion, though, still powered

---

Albion 5
  Allen (3)
  Nicholls
  Lee

Chelsea 2
  Bentley (2)

Ronnie Allen (standing, right) cracking home one of his three goals against Chelsea.

forward given the chance, and after a miskick by left half Derek Saunders, they added a fourth goal through Nicholls, who raced clear, dribbled neatly round the keeper and netted past full-back Stan Willemse who had dropped back to cover.

After this, Albion produced their best form of the afternoon and seven minutes from time, after Reg Ryan had robbed Ken Armstrong, George Lee raced in and his trusty left foot made the final score 5-2. This was the first time Albion had beaten Chelsea since September 1937. Following Wolves' 1-1 draw at Bolton, Albion's lead over the Molineux club at the top of the table was now four points (26-22). Huddersfield (also on 22) were, in fact, lying second.

Club News

Stan Rickaby received notice that he had been selected to represent the FA against the Army at Newcastle on 4 November.

Reg Ryan gained his thirteenth cap for the Republic of Ireland (and his fourteenth overall) when he played at left half against Luxembourg in Dublin.

Albion: Heath; Rickaby, Millard; Dudley, Dugdale, Barlow; Griffin, Ryan, Allen, Nicholls, Lee.

Chelsea: Robertson; Harris, Willemse; Armstrong, J. Saunders, D. Saunders; Parsons, McNichol, Bentley, Stubbs, Blunstone.

ALBION'S TOWER TOPPLED BY LATE SURGE

Date: Saturday 31 October 1953
Location: Bloomfield Road
Attendance: 27,104

Match title: League
Referee: Mr K.A. Collinge (Sale)

Stan Rickaby came through a late test to make his 150th first-team appearance for Albion, while captain Len Millard was having his 300th League outing as Vic Buckingham named an unchanged team for the third game running. Blackpool, just above the halfway mark in the table, fielded their England duo of Stanley Matthews and Stan Mortensen, and played with the wind during the first half.

However, it was the visitors who looked the more aggressive in the early stages and Johnny Nicholls' shot, from George Lee's low cross, grazed the top of the bar. Norman Heath saved brilliantly at the feet of Alan Brown as he raced onto a Matthews pass, and at the other end George Farm did likewise from Nicholls. The 27,000 plus crowd was enjoying every moment of the action, and on fourteen minutes Blackpool took the lead. Matthews, out on the right, teased and tormented Ray Barlow before whipping over a precise centre which Mortensen headed home from six yards.

Albion hit back and seven minutes later Allen equalised. His low shot from a left-wing clearance was mishandled by Farm, who scrambled on all fours as the ball trickled over the line. Allen then fired straight into Farm's arms when well placed. Eddie Shimwell cleared off the line from Barlow and Blackpool's Ernie Taylor struck the outside of a post – all before half-time.

It was cut and thrust at the start of the second period. Allen and Nicholls both failed to control the ball when in good positions, Jimmy Dudley fired narrowly wide and Mortensen and Bill Perry both had chances for the Seasiders. But with fifteen minutes remaining, and a draw looking the likely outcome, Blackpool reclaimed the lead against the run of play.

There seemed no danger as the ball bounced upwards inside the Albion penalty area, but Taylor somehow got his foot higher than anyone else and netted with a spectacular hook-shot. Rickaby then charged fifty yards upfield, only to see his angled drive skim past the far upright. In the eighty-third minute, with Albion pressing for an equaliser, Blackpool went 3-1 in front and again it was little Ernie Taylor who found space to shoot past Heath. It was all over a minute later when Brown netted from ten yards after the Baggies' defence had been spreadeagled by some fine wing-play from Matthews.

So, Albion's excellent run of away results (seven straight wins) came to a stuttering end at Bloomfield Road, but they would soon bounce back! On this very same day Wolves beat Preston North End 1-0 at Molineux to close up to within two points of Albion at the top of the table (26-24).

Blackpool 4
  Mortensen
  Taylor (2)
  Brown

Albion 1
  Allen

Club News

Stan Rickaby, after some excellent displays at right-back, was named in the full England team to play Northern Ireland at Goodison Park on 11 November. He had been ready to play for the FA XI against the Army at Newcastle on 4 November but was withdrawn at the last minute and replaced by Jeff Hall of Birmingham City.

Joe Kennedy won a short flying billiards tournament with Harry Ashley (reserve team trainer/coach) runner-up.

Albion's Central League side beat Bury 2-0, Wilf Carter and Allan Crowshaw the scorers.

West Bromwich Transport Authority announced that they would be putting on around 100 special buses to take supporters to Molineux for the local derby with Wolves on 14 November.

Above left: Blackpool goalkeeper George Farm pulled off some smart saves. *Above right:* Stan Rickaby, making his 150th appearance for Albion, found Bill Perry a handful at times.

Blackpool: Farm; Shimwell, Garrett; Fenton, Johnston, Robinson; Matthews, Taylor, Mortensen, Brown, Perry.

Albion: Heath; Rickaby, Millard; Dudley, Dugdale, Barlow; Griffin, Ryan, Allen, Nicholls, Lee.

BARLOW'S 40-YARD BLOCKBUSTER

Date: Saturday 7 November 1953
Location: The Hawthorns
Attendance: 37,704

Match title: League
Referee: Mr J. McCann (Preston)

Albion manager Vic Buckingham recalled centre half Joe Kennedy for the home game with bottom club Sunderland. He had not figured in a first-team match since February 1953, when he was injured during the 2-1 victory over Manchester City at The Hawthorns. The visitors were minus Ray Daniel and Trevor Ford, and the England cricketer Willie Watson was brought in at right-back.

Albion almost scored after just twenty-five seconds but Ronnie Allen, eight yards out, completely missed his kick after being set up by George Lee. Len Millard headed a Billy Elliott corner away from under his own crossbar; Ray Barlow had a long-range shot charged down and Allen lobbed fractionally over the top.

Sunderland, matching Albion kick for kick, came close again on twenty minutes when Heath somehow finger-tipped Tommy Wright's low drive round a post. Soon afterwards Heath was in action again, saving from Kirtley. But the Albion keeper was lucky when Len Shackleton's drive hit an upright and went beyond the goal. Allen's overhead kick was not matched by Reg Ryan's control in front of goal, and as half-time approached centre half Fred Hall took another powerful right-footed shot from the Baggies' centre forward on the chest.

A white ball was brought into play at the start of the second half and first into action was Kennedy, who stopped a run from Wright with a timely tackle. Wright was then pulled up for offside (a close decision) before Nicholls' effort went for a corner off the outstretched leg of Watson. On sixty-three minutes the deadlock was broken when Barlow, taking a short pass from Rickaby, strode forward. Forty yards from goal he let fly and saw the ball fly past keeper Ted McNeill high into the net at the Brummie Road end of the ground. A wonderful strike, a real crackerjack, reminiscent of the fireworks earlier in the week!

Brief incursions by the Sunderland wingers kept Albion's back division alert, but it was virtually game over on seventy-three minutes when Lee made it 2-0. Barlow dribbled his way into the crowded penalty area and fed his left-winger whose thunderous shot entered the net via the angle of crossbar and upright. Just afterwards McNeill stopped a piledriver from Nicholls, and at the death another mighty drive from Man of the Match Barlow smashed against the angle of bar and upright. Kennedy came through the match with flying colours, Heath performed exceedingly well in goal and Allen was always threatening. Albion were back on track and ready for the battle of the giants at Molineux! Wolves drew 3-3 at lowly Middlesbrough and therefore found themselves three points behind Albion (28-25). Huddersfield had twenty-three points and Burnley twenty-two.

Albion 2	**Sunderland 0**
Barlow	
Lee	

42

Albion's outstanding half-back line of Ray Barlow, Joe Kennedy and Jimmy Dudley, playing together for the first time in 1953/54, helped nullify the threat of Len Shackleton and company.

Club News

The president of the Football League, Mr Arthur Drewery CBE JP attended the Albion-Sunderland League game.

Stan Rickaby duly collected his first full cap when he helped England beat Northern Ireland 3-1 at Goodison Park.

Jimmy Dudley was named in the Scotland XI to play The Army at Goodison Park on 18 November and a week later Reg Ryan, if fit and released, would play for the Republic of Ireland against France in Paris.

Ronnie Allen and Freddie Cox, both fully qualified FA coaches, visited Malvern College to pass some of their footballing experience onto students.

Derek Kevan was chosen to represent the Army against Cambridge University (at Cambridge) on 19 November.

On 12 November, an Albion XI beat Oxford University 7-1 in a friendly, Elfed Evans scoring a hat-trick. Dr Tommy Thompson, who helped form the famous Pegasus amateur team, was manager of the Oxford University side.

Albion: Heath; Rickaby, Millard; Dudley, Kennedy, Barlow; Griffin, Ryan, Allen, Nicholls, Lee.

Sunderland: McNeil; Watson, Hudgell; Anderson, Hall, Aitken; Bingham, Shackleton, Wright, Kirtley, Elliott.

LUCKY GOAL WINS BLACK COUNTRY DERBY

Date: Saturday 14 November 1953
Location: Molineux
Attendance: 56,590

Match title: League
Referee: Mr F. Cowen (Manchester)

This was Joe Kennedy's 150th first-team appearance for unchanged Albion. Meanwhile Wolves, unbeaten in fourteen matches, were without Peter Broadbent (injured) and Bill Slater who was on duty with the England amateur team. This Black Country encounter, even today, is one of the big games of the season and the second-largest League crowd ever to assemble at Molineux, almost 56,600, saw a very tight and enthralling contest which was decided as early as the fifth minute with a fluke goal from Wolves' left-winger Jimmy Mullen.

Both teams had attacked down the wings early on before Stan Rickaby dallied far too long on the ball. Johnny Hancocks robbed him, fed Mullen who, finding enough space, swung his leg and curled over a hopeful cross (some called it a half-shot-cum-half-centre). Unfortunately, Albion's keeper Norman Heath, who had been in excellent form all season, completely misjudged the flight of the ball and could only collect it ruefully from the back of the net as the Wolves supporters and players celebrated.

Wolves, whose plan was based on close marking and quick tackling, upset Albion's elaborate short-passing technique, but they failed to penetrate a tight defence, while at the other end Ronnie Allen and Reg Ryan both got in strong shots at Bert Williams. After that early goal, the first half was fairly evenly matched, but it was Albion who took control of proceedings after the interval. They bombarded the Wolves goal for fifteen minutes, and during that time a splendid header from Allen fell narrowly wide, while Nicholls was only inches off-target with a snap-shot after some smart work by Ray Barlow. Admittedly, at times Albion chose to make six passes when three would have sufficed, but they created more chances than their opponents and were desperately unlucky not to score.

Gradually though, they got bogged down in midfield as Wolves took over. Wingers Hancocks and Mullen started to run up and down the touchlines like two whippets, keeping Albion's full-backs fully occupied, while Roy Swinbourne and Dennis Wilshaw in the middle were causing problems for Joe Kennedy and his colleagues. Twice Heath had to save at the feet of the former. Nevertheless, Allen was always a threat and he almost equalised in the eightieth minute with a fine diving header from Jimmy Dudley's cross. The ball beat Williams but bounced back into the keeper's arms as Nicholls moved in for the kill. Late on Bill Shorthouse cleared from six yards after Williams had parried another Allen effort. Wolves took the points but Albion matched them kick for kick and had the two best players on the pitch in Barlow and Allen. The referee wasn't bad either – one of the best seen at Molineux for years, said one supporter! This was the first time

Wolverhamptons Wanderers 1
Mullen

Albion 0

WOLVERHAMPTON WANDERERS v. ALBION

Albion had failed to score in a League game since 11 April 1953 (twenty matches ago). After this setback, Albion's lead at the top of the First Division was cut to just one point (28-27) and there were still twenty-four matches left to play.

Club News

After some superb displays, wing half Jimmy Dudley was honoured by the Scottish FA (*v.* The Army) at Everton's Goodison Park ground on 18 November.

Albion's reserve side slipped to below halfway in the Central League after losing 2-1 at home to Blackburn Rovers.

On Wednesday 18 November, Albion signed Durham County right-winger Tommy Watson on a month's trial.

Also on 18 November, both Ronnie Allen and Joe Kennedy sat with the 'reserves' and watched England humiliated 6-3 by Hungary at Wembley in a friendly international.

Wolves and England goalkeeper Bert Williams smothers the ball as George Lee slides in past Bill Shorthouse. The other two Albion players featured are Frank Griffin (left) and Ronnie Allen.

Wolverhampton Wanderers: Williams; Short, Pritchard; Baxter, Shorthouse, Wright; Hancocks, Stockin, Swinbourne, Wilshaw, Mullen.

Albion: Heath; Rickaby, Millard; Dudley, Kennedy, Barlow; Griffin, Ryan, Allen, Nicholls, Lee.

ALLEN FINDS LEAKS IN POROUS DEFENCE

Date: Saturday 21 November 1953   **Match title:** League
Location: The Hawthorns   **Referee:** Mr J.B. Jackson (Watford)
Attendance: 39,618

Stan Rickaby was missing from Albion's line-up for the game against Cardiff City. He was injured at Wolves and failed to respond to treatment. It ended a run of 143 consecutive League appearances for the right-back. Cardiff had already conceded twenty-eight goals and on paper their defence wasn't all that secure.

Albion set off like a train and had three shots at goal in the first two minutes, two of them from Ronnie Allen who was soon to emphasise to the selectors what a big mistake they had made by not including him in the team against Puskas & Co. However, before that, the Welsh club surprisingly took the lead when Jack Chisholm, left on his own at the far post, headed home from a deep free-kick by Dougie Blair. Johnny Nicholls should have equalised immediately but sent his effort into the crowd. Thankfully, on fourteen minutes, George Lee's shot cannoned off a defender (Blair) and dropped to the feet of Allen who simply tapped the ball home from six yards. Norman Heath kept out a rasping drive from Wilf Grant before Allen made it 2-1 on twenty-eight minutes, netting from close range after some neat build-up play involving four players. With Cardiff back-pedalling, the Albion

Albion 6
  Allen (4)
  Nicholls (2)

Cardiff City 1
  Chisholm

centre forward completed his hat-trick ten minutes before the interval, cracking home Reg Ryan's pass with great efficiency.

With the Cardiff defence at sixes and sevens, Allen swooped again six minutes into the second half, netting with a daisy-cutter from distance, keeper Ron Howells looking bemused the ball went past him. Nicholls, Frank Griffin and Lee all had openings after that, while Cardiff's right-back Alan Harrington knocked the ball against his own upright with a misdirected backpass. In the seventy-ninth minute Nicholls got himself on the scoresheet with Albion's fifth goal, and four minutes later he added to his tally by sliding home Griffin's pinpoint centre. Albion continued to drive forward, and in the last five minutes had four more shots on target, all of which could and should have found the net. It was an excellent all-round performance by 'Buckingham's Beauties' and, as one newspaper headline stated, 'Albion Are Back'. This victory, Albion's biggest at home in terms of goals scored since they beat Bradford 7-1 in April 1949, certainly made up for the huge disappointment of losing at Molineux. Wolves won 2-0 at Charlton and remained a point behind Albion (30-29) at the head of the table. Huddersfield (25 points) lay third, ahead of Burnley (24).

Club News

On 21 November, Albion's reserves lost 3-0 at Blackpool.

Albion: Heath; S. Williams, Millard; J. Dudley, Kennedy, Barlow; Griffin, Ryan, Allen, Nicholls, Lee.

Cardiff City: Howells; Harrington, Sullivan; Baker, Montgomery, Blair; Tiddy, F. Dudley, Grant, Chisholm, Edwards.

A BATTLING PERFORMANCE FROM ALBION

Date: Saturday 28 November 1953
Location: Maine Road
Attendance: 40,753

Match title: League
Referee: Mr A. Brown (Middlesbrough)

Stan Rickaby returned at right-back in a game that saw Norman Heath make his 150th appearance for Albion (including wartime), and the goalkeeper had to be at his very best to prevent a defeat at Maine Road. He pulled off five superb saves, three late in the second half, as City strived to get something out of a game they believed they should have never lost!

It was a tough encounter. Albion started very well, and George Lee hit the woodwork after just thirty seconds, and a minute later shot straight across the face of the City goal. The home side, in reply, also launched an early attack that saw Johnny Hart's shot fumbled by Norman Heath, but the goalkeeper recovered to clear his lines. City took the lead on ten minutes when Roy Paul's free-kick was punched out by Heath. The ball fell to Don Revie fifteen yards out, who controlled it with one foot and drove it straight into the net with the other. This put Albion on their mettle, and a lovely interpassing movement involving Reg Ryan and Ray Barlow resulted in Ronnie Allen firing in a shot at City's German-born keeper Bert Trautmann. On nineteen minutes Albion equalised when Ryan and Allen exchanged passes to send Lee clear twenty yards from goal. His left-footed half-volley was misjudged by Trautmann, who thought the ball was going over the bar, but to his disbelief it dipped viciously at the last second and ended up in the back of the net.

Albion gradually took control of the match and should have taken the lead but for a rather weak finish from Johnny Nicholls and an excellent save by Trautmann. On twenty-four minutes they did go ahead. A lovely pass from Jimmy Dudley found Ryan on the right. A square ball to Nicholls was flicked on to Allen who was racing into the City danger zone. As cool as a cucumber, the in-form striker buried his shot beyond the keeper. 2-1 to the Baggies.

Before the interval Trautmann saved superbly from Frank Griffin and a Barlow header, and Nicholls was tackled eight yards from goal. At the other end both Roy Clarke and Hart had shots charged down and Len Millard nipped in to thwart the latter with a last-ditch clearance.

Against the run of play City came back and equalised on forty-seven minutes when Johnny Hart, three yards out, netted from a clever running centre by the impressive and lively Bobby Cunliffe, Heath just failing to incept the cross. Albion, though disturbed to concede when they did, regained their composure, pushed an extra man forward and regained the lead with a terrific sixty-first minute goal from Nicholls, who headed home

Manchester City 2	Albion 3
Revie	Lee
Hart	Allen
	Nicholls

Allen's cross with great skill from five yards. After that Griffin, Allen, Ryan and Nicholls had chances to increase the lead, but it was Heath who stole the show, keeping out fine efforts from Hart and Cunliffe, while Jimmy Meadows sent a drive fizzing over the Albion bar as City pressed for an equaliser they thought they deserved. Heath, Joe Kennedy, Ray Barlow and Ronnie Allen (once more) shone for Albion, while Roy Paul and Revie were outstanding for City. This victory took Albion onto 32 points, one more than Wolves, who kept in touch with a comprehensive 4-1 home win over Sheffield Wednesday. Huddersfield (27 points) were still third.

Club News

Albion defeated Boldmere St Michael's 7-2 in a third round FA Youth Cup-tie at The Hawthorns on 28 November. Brian Whitehouse scored four of the goals.

Arthur Loach, who played for Albion in the 1886 FA Cup Final v. Blackburn Rovers, celebrated his ninetieth birthday on 29 November.

After losing three games on the trot, Albion's Second XI got back to winning ways with a 2-1 home victory over Barnsley, Elfed Evans and Wilf Carter the goalscorers.

 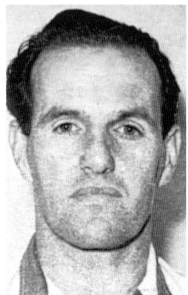

Above left: Ronnie Allen was again on target at Maine Road. *Above right:* Left-winger George Lee also found the City net.

Manchester City: Trautmann; Branagan, Little; Revie, Ewing, Paul; Anders, Hart, Meadows, Clarke, Cunliffe.
Albion: Heath; Rickaby, Millard; Dudley, Kennedy, Barlow; Griffin, Ryan, Allen, Nicholls, Lee.

PORTSMOUTH SNATCH LATE WINNER

Date: Saturday 5 December 1953
Location: The Hawthorns
Attendance: 29,623

Match title: League
Referee: Mr J.C. Pollard (Cambridge)

Albion, again at full strength, were quietly confident of extending their unbeaten home run to six matches when Portsmouth visited The Hawthorns on a cold winter's afternoon. The Baggies had enjoyed some great victories over Pompey in recent years, winning 3-0, 5-0, 5-0 and 2-0 in successive seasons since gaining promotion in 1949. Pompey, struggling at fourth from bottom in the table, had already lost ten of their nineteen matches and had conceded over fifty goals – the most in Division One, whereas Albion had scored the most, fifty-six. But as so often happens in football, a shock result occurred as Albion slumped to a 3-2 defeat – only their second at home all season. Nothing went right for Albion. They didn't play badly; far from it. They created twice as many chances as Portsmouth but some sloppy defensive play cost them dearly.

Pompey, under pressure early on, recovered to take an eighth-minute lead, inside right Johnny Gordon scoring their first goal at The Hawthorns since January 1938 after a misplaced header by Joe Kennedy. Albion recovered and dictated play for long periods up to half-time. Twice Johnny Nicholls was sent clear but each time he was denied a goal by keeper first Platt and then an outstretched foot of centre half Duggie Reid who had a splendid game. George Lee went close, as did Ronnie Allen right on the half-time whistle with a cracking drive which was tipped round the post by Platt. Gordon (again) and the ex-Charlton striker Charlie Vaughan had chances for the visitors, Heath saving quite brilliantly from the latter's sharply angled drive.

Ten minutes into the second half Pompey increased their lead. A free-kick was headed goalwards by Vaughan; Heath dived and pushed the ball onto a post, only for it to rebound to Peter Harris who netted from all of two yards. Albion complained, to no avail, that Harris was already offside when Vaughan headed the ball.

Through hard work and grim determination Albion battled back and after a couple of near misses, they drew level with two goals in the space of four minutes just before the hour mark. On fifty-seven minutes Nicholls, who had come so close to scoring in the first period, reduced the deficit after a sweet flowing move involving four players and five passes. Then on sixty minutes Allen headed home from almost on the goal line after Frank Griffin's cross-cum-shot had been partially stopped by keeper Platt. Albion continued to press forward; right-back Stan Rickaby fired just over and Allen put an effort wide.

But with the game seemingly destined to end in a draw and with the referee checking his watch, Ray Barlow, who had been by far the best player on the pitch, made a tragic error, miskicking inside his own penalty area and allowing Gordon to snatch a dramatic

Albion 2	Portsmouth 3
Nicholls	Gordon (2)
Allen	Harris

late winner. After three months as top dogs, this defeat meant that Albion slipped down to second place in the Division following Wolves' 3-2 win at Tottenham. The men from Molineux now had 33 points to Albion's 32.

Club News

Freddie Cox missed a penalty as Albion's reserve side conceded a goal in the last minute when losing 1-0 at Sheffield United.

It was announced, via the club, that three players – Wilf Carter, Gerry Summers and goalkeeper Reg Davies – would all be demobbed from the forces around Christmas time.

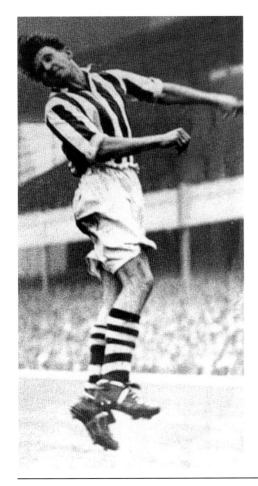

Ray Barlow played splendidly and didn't deserve to be on the losing side.

Albion: Heath; Rickaby, Millard; Dudley, Kennedy, Barlow; Griffin, Ryan, Allen, Nicholls, Lee.

Portsmouth: Platt; Gunter, Mansell; Phillips, Reid, Dickinson; Harris, Gordon, Vaughan, Hunt, Henderson.

ALBION BACK ON TOP

Date: Saturday 12 December 1953
Location: Highbury
Attendance: 55,269

Match title: League
Referee: Mr B.M. Griffiths (Newport)

Following the double disappointment of suffering a home defeat and losing the top spot in Division One on the same day, unchanged Albion went for the jugular from the start at Highbury and took the lead after just fifty seconds. After an astute passing movement involving three Albion players, Arsenal defender Bill Dodgin's clearance hit Reg Ryan and rebounded to Johnny Nicholls who side-footed home past keeper Jack Kelsey. It was as simple as that! Keeping up the pressure, Albion should have scored again ten minutes later, but Reg Ryan's tame effort was blocked. Doug Lishman had the Gunners' first shot at goal, but Norman Heath saved comfortably, and then Albion doubled their score on fifteen minutes. A judicious Ronnie Allen through ball found Nicholls, who raced into the penalty area and fired a right-foot rocket high into the roof of the net via the crossbar, keeper Kelsey standing practically still, arms raised, stunned by the sheer speed and power of the shot.

Doug Lishman then reduced the arrears on twenty-two minutes with a perfectly guided header from Bill Dickson's well-executed forward chip. Just after this goal, Albion's right half Jimmy Dudley suffered a nasty cut to his mouth (after being accidentally kicked in the face) and had to leave the field for a good quarter of an hour to have four stitches inserted in the wound. Arsenal capitalised on their good fortune and pinned Albion's defence back. With the Baggies still down to ten men, Lishman equalised with a cross-shot from the left side of the penalty area after being put through by Cliff Holton, the ball taking a slight deflection off Len Millard before fizzing past Heath's right hand.

With Dudley back in the action, Heath then saved at the feet of Holton, receiving a crack on the head for his bravery, while at the other end of the field a splendid lob from Allen bounced on top of the crossbar twice before dropping behind the goal.

There were more thrills and spills in the second half. Ryan and Nicholls both missed sitters for Albion in the space of five minutes after pull-backs from Allen and Lee, and Don Roper and Holton also blazed wide for the Gunners as the play ebbed to and fro. The pace began to tell on certain players and three were treated for cramp in less than a minute. Heath flung himself sideways to save brilliantly from Lishman, and Millard somehow scrambled another Arsenal effort off the line.

Albion came on strongly at the end and with Arsenal reeling, the last chance of the game fell to Allen, but Kelsey matched his well-struck shot with an exceptionally fine save. A draw was a fair result to a magnificent game of football, much appreciated by the huge Highbury crowd. Wolves were surprisingly beaten 2-1 at home by Burnley and with this point at Highbury Albion regained top spot.

Arsenal 2
 Lishman (2)

Albion 2
 Nicholls (2)

Club News

On Monday 14 December the draw for the third round of the FA Cup was made and Albion were paired with Chelsea at The Hawthorns. Albion and the London club had met four times in the fourth round the previous season, the Stamford Bridge side eventually winning 4-0 in a third replay at Highbury. In the FA Youth Cup Albion's youngsters drew Sunderland at Roker Park.

Elfed Evans scored a hat-trick (including a penalty) as Albion's reserves beat Huddersfield 5-1 at The Hawthorns to move up to tenth and above Aston Villa in the Central League. Albion Colts won 4-0 under floodlights at Kidderminster on 9 December to take over top spot in the Midland Mid-Week League. In a Handsworth League game, fifteen-year-old John Moore scored seven goals as Albion's fifth team beat British Road Services 12-0 at Dudley.

Arsenal's Welsh international goalkeeper Jack Kelsey dives at the feet of Ronnie Allen.

Arsenal: Kelsey; Wills, Smith; Dickson, Dodgin, Mercer; Roper, Logie, Holton, Lishman, Marden.

Albion: Heath; Rickaby, Millard; Dudley, Kennedy, Barlow; Griffin, Ryan, Allen, Nicholls, Lee.

UNLUCKY LOSERS

Date: Saturday 19 December 1953
Location: Burnden Park
Attendance: 35,198

Match title: League
Referee: Mr G. McCabe (Sheffield)

Fielding the team that earned a very useful point at Highbury, Albion found it tough going during the first quarter of an hour at Burnden Park against a strong, resolute and determined Bolton Wanderers side who were lying fifth in the table yet were without a win in five games. As early as the first minute, however, Reg Ryan had a shot cleared off the line. From the resulting corner Ronnie Allen cracked the ball onto a post and then saw it zip across the face of the goal, strike the other upright and bounce to safety. Then the home side got going. Ray Barlow headed away a dangerous cross from Ray Parry and keeper Heath was at full stretch to keep out a long-range shot from Willie Moir. Joe Kennedy got the better of Nat Lofthouse in another heading duel as Bolton dictated the play.

Six chances, three by either side, were missed in the space of ten minutes midway through the half. Ryan, Allen and Nicholls (when faced with a one-on-one situation) were the Albion culprits, while Lofthouse fluffed Bolton's easiest opening.

Though not reaching the sort of form they produced at Highbury, Albion certainly had far more of the play between the thirtieth and forty-fifth minutes, and Bolton keeper Stan Hanson saved well from both Allen and Johnny Nicholls. Albion went in at the break knowing they should have been ahead, having had the better of the first forty-five minutes.

Early in the second half a Nicholls shot was diverted wide by full-back Tommy Banks, and Alan Beards, who was making his first appearance of the season for Bolton, fired too close to Heath from ten yards. Lofthouse then headed against the bar and saw the rebound bounce off Heath and go behind for a corner.

On fifty-six minutes Bolton took the lead. Beards got away from Rickaby and crossed for Ray Parry to fire in a shot that Heath knocked out to Lofthouse, who scored from six yards. Nine minutes later it was 2-0. Johnny Wheeler moved forward to take a pass on the edge of the penalty area. His shot was straight at Heath but the ball rebounded out and the Bolton right half ran up to head into the net over the prostrate keeper.

Allen struck a post as Albion hit back, while another Lofthouse header was saved by Heath, and soon afterwards the robust England international struck the bar. In a grandstand finish Ryan scored for Albion on seventy-seven minutes (after a neat one-two) and then saw Barlow's low shot saved by the diving Hanson, while Jimmy Dudley's effort flew over the top as the game went into the final minute. It was a frustrating afternoon for the Baggies, who certainly didn't deserve to lose. Thanks to a 3-1 home win over

---

Bolton Wanderers 2
Lofthouse
Wheeler

Albion 1
Ryan

Pre-Christmas shooting practice at The Hawthorns: trainer Arthur Fitton (back to camera) puts Ronnie Allen, Reg Ryan (shooting) and Johnny Nicholls through their paces against goalkeeper Norman Heath.

Manchester City, Wolves went back to the top of the First Division table with 35 points to Albion's 33. Huddersfield Town (27 points) were drifting off the pace.

Club News

Albion's second team beat Bolton 1-0 at The Hawthorns, Elfed Evans the goalscorer.

As Don Howe, Brian Whitehouse and goalkeeper Geoff Barnsley were preparing to join the forces for National Service, three were ready to come home – Wilf Carter, Reg Davies and Gerry Summers.

Chelsea claimed their full entitlement of 25 per cent of the tickets for the third round FA Cup-tie at The Hawthorns on 9 January, thus guaranteeing, no matter what the weather, a gate in excess of 35,000.

Bolton Wanderers: Hanson; Ball, Banks; Wheeler, Barrass, Bell; Holden, Moir, Lofthouse, Parry, Beards.

Albion: Heath; Rickaby, Millard; Dudley, Kennedy, Barlow; Griffin, Ryan, Allen, Nicholls, Lee.

A CHRISTMAS DAY SPECIAL

Date: Friday 25 December 1953
Location: The Hawthorns
Attendance: 30,390

Match title: League
Referee: Mr A. Holland (Barnsley)

With no bus service or trams and only a few special trains running to The Hawthorns Halt railway station, it was amazing that over 30,000 fans attended this Christmas Day morning game against third from bottom Liverpool (kick-off 11 a.m.). Albion, unchanged yet again (testament to the efforts of the training and coaching staff) and with Frank Griffin making his 100th first-team appearance for the club, started strongly and scored three goals in the first fifteen minutes, during which time they gave a brilliant exhibition of all-out attacking football. After that though, the team slipped out of gear and were no better than Liverpool. Even the fans started to moan when passes went astray. After the visitors had got back into the game at 3-2, the Baggies picked up the momentum and although not at their best, ran out convincing winners in the end.

As early as the first minute Ronnie Allen was denied a goal by a superb one-handed save by keeper Russell Crossley, but in Albion's next attack, aimed down the Liverpool left, Griffin's perfectly lobbed centre was headed home by Johnny Nicholls. A down-the-middle thrust brought a second goal six minutes later. A quick interchange of passing between Ray Barlow and Allen resulted in the former cracking home a splendid shot from the inside right position. On the quarter-hour mark it was 3-0. Griffin, finding space, put over a square centre that Crossley got his hands to but couldn't hold, the ball falling behind him into the net. A slight Albion relaxation enabled Liverpool to get back into the game, and after Reg Ryan's effort was disallowed Alan A'Court, a menacing winger throughout, created a goal on forty-one minutes. He fed Sammy Smyth (ex-Wolves) who got in a shot which seemed to be going wide, only to see Stan Rickaby needlessly handle the ball. Up stepped Ray Lambert to crack the penalty beyond Heath. Allen took a knock on the head and for a short while occupied the right-wing berth (to regain his composure) and he almost scored with a deep cross which keeper Crossley, a yard or so off his line, just managed to palm over the bar. Albion goalkeeper Norman Heath was also injured, taking a kick in the teeth.

Liverpool – who were without their influential, all-purpose forward Billy Liddell – started the second half well and A'Court, later to play for England, almost made it 3-2. Albion found themselves under pressure and couldn't seem to raise their game, so much so that Liverpool had three chances in the space of ten minutes but missed them all. On seventy-one minutes, A'Court suddenly cut inside to make it 3-2. At this juncture Albion were rocking, but they slowly and deliberately drove the visitors back, regained control of the match and scored a fourth goal on eighty-four minutes courtesy of a smart header

Albion 5	Liverpool 2
Griffin (2), Barlow	Lambert (pen)
Nicholls, Allen	A'Court

by Allen from Nicholls' cross. Allen, however, hurt his neck when scoring and had to be carried off. Albion, now firmly back in control, netted a fifth goal three minutes from time. A brilliant dribble forward by Ray Barlow ended when the left half teed up Griffin, who scored with a well-directed right-foot shot.

Barlow was once again Man of the Match while new signing Geoff Twentyman played very well for Liverpool, as did Welsh international Lambert, despite having to mark the impressive Griffin. One newspaper cutting stated: 'A satisfactory win, but Albion must not slacken off ... it could be fatal.' Another wrote: 'Five goals but Albion had their failings ... They ran into an inexplicably poor spell which might easily have cost them the points.' This was the third game in a row that Liverpool had conceded five goals, and the eighth time they had let in four or more in a match during the twenty-four games they had played in the season. Albion went back to the top of the table with this victory, as Wolves had lost 2-1 at home to Aston Villa twenty-four hours earlier. Albion had now accumulated thirty-five points, the same number as Wolves, but had a far better goal average.

Club News

When claiming their fifth goal against Liverpool Albion brought their tally for the season to sixty-six, precisely the same number they scored in all their forty-two League games in 1952/53.

A board meeting at The Hawthorns in 1953: manager Vic Buckingham is seated on the extreme left, chairman Major H. Wilson Keys is at the head of the table and club secretary Eph Smith is on the right, next to future chairman Mr Jim Gaunt.

Albion: Heath; Rickaby, Millard; Dudley, Kennedy, Barlow; Griffin, Ryan, Allen, Nicholls, Lee.
Liverpool: Crossley; Taylor, Lambert; Wilkinson, Twentyman, Paisley; Jackson, Smyth, Bimpson, Smith, A'Court.

ANFIELD STALEMATE

Date: Saturday 26 December 1953
Location: Anfield
Attendance: 51,167

Match title: League
Referee: Mr A. Holland (Barnsley)

Albion travelled to Anfield with an unchanged team, Ronnie Allen and Norman Heath both reporting fit after their respective head and mouth injuries suffered at The Hawthorns twenty-four hours earlier. In contrast, the Liverpool boss Don Welsh, the former Charlton Athletic outside right, made three changes, bringing in goalkeeper Dave Underwood, who was signed just before Christmas from Watford, and introducing full-back Frank Lock and inside right John Evans who were both recruited a day or two earlier from the manager's former club. Underwood, in fact, started the game with a heavily strapped right thigh which ultimately disrupted his kicking.

The return fixture was a terrifically exciting affair and the 0-0 scoreline was a complete misrepresentation of the splendid attacking play that both teams crammed into the ninety minutes. Despite a muddy pitch, there was action at both ends of the field from the first to the last whistle and the respective goalkeepers certainly earned their wages with some brilliant saves, Albion's Norman Heath pulling off two quite unbelievable stops to deny first Alan A'Court and then centre forward Louis Bimpson, who was later responsible for the miss of the match, putting the ball wide from just a yard out! Both sides had three one-on-one situations, Allen and Nicholls (twice) being the Albion players who failed to find the net.

Albion were perhaps the better team in the first half and should, realistically speaking, have gone in with at least a two-goal advantage, although Allen was unlucky to have one effort ruled out for offside after the goalkeeper had punched Ray Barlow's drive to the feet of the centre forward.

Albion's defence had to work much harder in the second period as the home side, backed by a vociferous crowd, attacked more and more as the game went on, Heath pulling off another miraculous save from Bimpson and Joe Kennedy clearing off his own line. It was a point earned not lost by Albion after their first goalless draw, at home or away, in League football since October 1952, fifty-five matches ago. Wolves turned the tables on Villa, winning the return fixture at Aston 2-1, and as a result leap-frogged Albion to move back into top spot by a point (37-36).

Club News
Stuart Williams was one of the few footballers to spend Christmas at home – he was reserve for the first team when Liverpool visited The Hawthorns and then skippered the reserves on Boxing Day, deputising for the injured Harold Wright in a 1-0 victory over the Merseysiders, Elfed Evans' penalty proving to be the winner in front of almost 5,000 spectators.

Liverpool 0   **Albion 0**

Right: The matchday programme cover. *Below right:* Goalkeeper Norman Heath was in excellent form at Anfield. *Below:* Len 'The Agitator' Millard, Albion's consistent captain and left-back.

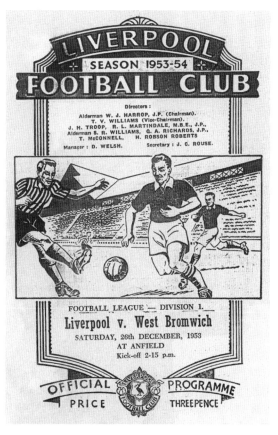

Liverpool: Underwood; Lambert, Lock; Wilkinson, Twentyman, Paisley; Jackson, Smyth, Bimpson, Evans, A'Court.

Albion: Heath; Rickaby, Millard; Dudley, Kennedy, Barlow; Griffin, Ryan, Allen, Nicholls, Lee.

OVERHEAD STUNNER FROM ALLEN

Date: Saturday 2 January 1954
Location: The Hawthorns
Attendance: 20,306

Match title: League
Referee: Mr W. Ratcliffe (Leek)

On a fog-bound, frosty afternoon, unchanged Albion had to work exceptionally hard (especially in the second half) to overcome a resilient and stubborn but very useful Preston side (minus Tom Finney) before completing their second double of the season. During the first forty-five minutes Albion played some sparkling football and scored twice despite a hard and in parts very bumpy pitch, but then, for no explicable reason, they eased up after the interval, conceded two sloppy goals and in the end were hanging on by their bootlaces as the visitors threw caution to the wind as they went in search of an equaliser.

Albion's opening goal on thirty-one minutes was a real gem. Ray Barlow, who had a wonderful match and was wearing some special rubber-studded boots, took a throw in near the halfway line. Receiving the ball back from Nicholls, he then played it sideways to Len Millard who fed it back to Barlow as he made ground down the left. The big fellow swept menacingly past three opponents before whipping over a head-high cross, aimed towards Ronnie Allen. The Albion striker had his back to goal but suddenly flung himself upwards and with a marvellously executed overhead kick sent the ball flying into the net from fifteen yards. A magnificent goal – even Preston's keeper George Thompson applauded. Five minutes later Allen found the net again as Albion went 2-0 up, neatly heading home George Lee's measured cross from the left, the ball going in off a post.

The visibility had improved slightly as the second half got underway but play was still sloppy. After a surprise flourish by Preston and a long-range effort from Frank Griffin, Nicholls secured his twenty-third goal of the season with a brave diving header from a rapid left-wing run and centre by Lee to give Albion breathing space at 3-0 in the fifty-fourth minute. It should have been four soon afterwards but Reg Ryan hesitated and the chance was lost. Then came Preston's revival. Some unprofessional play led to Angus Morrison reducing the arrears on fifty-seven minutes, the winger putting away Bobby Foster's cross from the right with a fine left-foot shot. Albion, on the back foot, withstood some strong pressure and looked as if they were regaining control until Morrison struck again with a quarter of an hour to go. After a goalmouth mêlée, he steered his shot under Heath from six yards, the keeper just failing to get his hand on the ball as it crossed the line. Only two great tackles by Joe Kennedy prevented Foster and Charlie Wayman from getting through, and when the visiting centre forward did find space, he fired wide of the far post. Kennedy, though, was exceptional and he had Wayman practically in his pocket throughout the game. The crowd grew impatient; it was tense stuff, but after a penalty

Albion 3	**Preston North End 2**
Allen (2)	Morrison (2)
Nicholls	

claim by Ryan had been turned down, the referee sounded the final whistle and Albion had survived – just!

Albion were still second in the table with 38 points after Wolves had beaten Cardiff City 3-1 at Ninian Park.

Club News

Notices went out stating that if Albion's home third round FA Cup-tie with Chelsea ended in a draw, the replay would take place at Stamford Bridge the following Monday afternoon (kick-off 2 p.m.). Trains to London would leave Dudley Port, Oldbury & Bromford Lane, Smethwick and Birmingham New Street stations at various times during the morning of the game and the return fare would be 16s 6d (82½p) from Dudley Port and 15s (75p) from Birmingham. Albion supporters would be allocated 500 seat tickets for the match.

Only 115 spectators saw Stoke City reserves beat Albion reserves 1-0 in a Central League game at a foggy Victoria Ground on 2 January.

Frank Griffin's wife presented him with a son on 6 January.

Johnny Nicholls opened the
new year with another goal.

Albion: Heath; Rickaby, Millard; Dudley, Kennedy, Barlow; Griffin, Ryan, Allen, Nicholls, Lee.

Preston North End: Thompson; Cunningham, Walton; Docherty, Marston, Forbes; Jones, Foster, Wayman, Baxter, Morrison.

STAN'S THE MAN FOR ALBION

Date: Saturday 9 January 1954
Location: The Hawthorns
Attendance: 35,294 (receipts £34,801)

Match title: FA Cup third round
Referee: Mr R.E. Smith (Newport)

Albion manager Vic Buckingham was forced to make his first change in seven matches after Joe Kennedy declared himself unfit with a cold. Jimmy Dugdale took his place. His duels with Roy Bentley were a feature of the afternoon. Chelsea, unbeaten in nine games, had Chick Thomson in goal in place of Bill Robertson. The tie itself proved to be a gruelling affair, played on a very muddy pitch, slippery in places, which made ball control difficult at times. No quarter was given or asked and both sets of players slogged it out hammer and tongs for the whole ninety minutes. The tackling was fierce and Welsh referee Smith used his whistle frequently during a tight first half when both goalkeepers were forced into action on several occasions. Ray Barlow, who was brilliant throughout, grazed the crossbar on three occasions; Johnny Nicholls bent the Chelsea bar while Frank Griffin, whose trickery at times was worthy of Stanley Matthews, had a shot cleared off the line.

Albion, wearing white shirts and black shorts, had a half-chance in the very first minute, but the ball skidded off Reg Ryan's boot just as he was lining up a shot. Eric Parsons, the Chelsea right-winger, missed two seemingly easy chances while Ronnie Allen, closely marked all afternoon by future England manager Ron Greenwood, had three shots at goal (one a 20-yarder which was only inches wide). Ryan missed by a whisker and George Lee fired into the side netting – all before the break.

Early in the second half Allen shot narrowly wide and Roy Bentley's header at the other end was well held by Heath. Chances were few and far between as the rain came down and players tired, although Nicholls did strike a post with one close-range effort. Then Albion's right-back Stan Rickaby found some extra stamina. He had kept a close check on the speedy Frank Blunstone all afternoon, and with seven minutes remaining, chose to venture upfield prior to a free-kick being taken out on the right.

Frank Griffin played the ball high into the crowded penalty area. It was knocked out some twenty yards to Rickaby, who collected it in his stride, moved forward two paces and then rifled in a powerful right-footed drive, which could have hit the bar, gone fractionally over or just scraped underneath. In fact, it struck Greenwood on the head and flew into the net via the crossbar, giving keeper Thomson and the two full-backs on the line no chance whatsoever. Albion kept possession for the remaining few minutes before successfully claiming their place in the fourth round. Wolves were surprisingly dumped out of the FA Cup by Division Two Birmingham City, who won 2-1 at Molineux.

Albion 1   **Chelsea 0**
   Greenwood (og)

Right: Stan Rickaby – Albion's match-winner! *Far right:* Ray Barlow.

Club News

This was Albion's fifth FA Cup game against Chesea in twelve months. In January/February 1953, the teams played each other four times in the fourth round before the Londoners went through by virtue of a 4-0 victory at Highbury. During this sequence of matches, Vic Buckingham took over as manager at The Hawthorns.

On the Monday after the win over Chelsea, Albion heard over the radio that they would play Rotherham United at home in the fourth round of the FA Cup.

On 9 January Albion's sixth team beat Kingston Celtic 13-1 in Birmingham Youth Committee Junior League game. Barry Jeyes scored a double hat-trick.

On 12 January, Ronnie Allen's wife presented him with a son (Russell), who was later to join Albion as a player before going on to assist Tranmere Rovers and Mansfield Town.

Albion: Heath; Rickaby, Millard; Dudley, Dugdale, Barlow; Griffin, Ryan, Allen, Nicholls, Lee.

Chelsea: Thomson; Harris, Willemse; Armstrong, Greenwood, D. Saunders; Parsons, McNichol, Bentley, Stubbs, Blunstone.

ALBION SPURRED ON BY ALLEN

Date: Saturday 16 January 1954
Location: White Hart Lane
Attendance: 48,812

Match title: League
Referee: Mr F. Cowen (Manchester)

There was no Johnny Nicholls in Albion's attack. He was ruled out with a muscle strain in the small of his back and was replaced by Wilf Carter. And although Joe Kennedy had recovered from his cold, manager Vic Buckingham decided to keep faith with Jimmy Dugdale for the away game against his former club Spurs, who were perched in mid-table. And the young Liverpudlian played a blinder, completely blotting out the threat of Len Duquemin, the Londoners' joint-top scorer with nine goals.

Despite a very heavily sanded pitch which cut up badly as the game progressed, both teams played some superb football, especially during the first half, when Albion created more chances but Spurs had the easiest and missed them all, although credit must go to Dugdale (for one magnificent tackle) and to goalkeeper Norman Heath for three exceptionally fine saves, especially the one from Harry Clarke's header. His others were from Sonny Walters and Duquemin, who for once escaped the shackles of Dugdale.

Albion took the lead – which proved to be the winning goal – on thirty-five minutes. Stan Rickaby took the ball off England international George Robb and sent a long pass downfield to Ronnie Allen. He quickly switched the ball to Frank Griffin, who made ground before crossing to the far post where George Lee controlled the ball and then cleverly cut it back into the middle of the penalty area for the onrushing Allen, who had rapidly made ground, to unleash a powerful right-footed shot from twelve yards, the ball flying past goalkeeper Ted Ditchburn and the two covering full-backs, Alf Ramsey and Arthur Willis (all within a yard or so of the line) like a rocket. Spurs piled on the pressure as they searched for an equaliser but Albion's defence stood firm; and when they did get through Heath could not and would not be beaten.

Allen had a chance of a second goal in a rare breakaway, while Carter slipped at a crucial time when right in front of goal. After Spurs had also gone close, Lee, who had a fine game against Ramsey, fired across the face of the goal and Ryan skied a shot high into the crowd. Heath fisted a free-kick from Clarke round the angle of post and crossbar and almost immediately saved from Duquemin. Carter, demobbed twenty-four hours earlier, was never really in the game but he did create one last chance for Griffin, but his effort lacked direction. Allen, who covered acres of ground, shared the Man of the Match award with Dugdale. Albion, now up to 40 points, jumped over Wolves (39 points) after Cullis's men had been beaten 2-0 by Arsenal at Molineux. Huddersfield Town and Burnley, both with 34 points, were still in touch. The top four clubs had now completed twenty-seven League games.

Tottenham Hotspur 0	**Albion 1**
	Lee

TOTTENHAM HOTSPUR v. ALBION

Club News

On Wednesday 20 January, Johnny Nicholls played for the England Under-23 side against their Italian counterparts in a friendly international in Bologna. He partnered Chelsea's Frank Blunstone on the left-wing. The Italians won 3-0. Jimmy Dugdale was named as non-travelling reserve.

A crowd of over 48,000 was expected to attend Albion's fourth round FA Cup-tie with Rotherham as the Yorkshire club hinted it was bringing around 10,000 supporters to The Hawthorns.

While the seniors were winning at White Hart Lane, Albion's reserves lost 1-0 at home to Preston and the 'A' team crashed 6-1 at Rugby.

Spurs goalkeeper Ted Ditchburn smothers the ball as Frank Griffin closes in.

Tottenham Hotspur: Ditchburn; Ramsey, Willetts; Nicholson, Clarke, Burgess; Walters, Bennett, Duquemin, Baily, Robb.

Albion: Heath; Rickaby, Millard; Dudley, Dugdale, Barlow; Griffin, Ryan, Allen, Carter, Lee.

ALLEN MISSES HIS FIRST PENALTY

Date: Saturday 23 January 1954
Location: The Hawthorns
Attendance: 42,850

Match title: League
Referee: Mr F.L. Overton (Derby)

Johnny Nicholls was back in Albion's frontline for the visit of fourth-placed Burnley, who were fresh from a 5-0 hammering of Middlesbrough. Albion completely outplayed Burnley in the first half and did everything but score – although credit must be given to the visitors' goalkeeper Des Thompson, who pulled off three brilliant saves, two in quick succession, one a real rasping effort fired in by the 'Irish Tinker' Paddy Ryan.

A Ronnie Allen shot had the keeper beaten but was headed behind for a corner by Tommy Cummings, and then another fine left-footed drive from Ryan, who was falling backwards, almost slipped through Thompson's arms. Jimmy Dudley had a ripsnorter turned round the post, and how one of Allen's first-time hook shots was cleared to safety remains a mystery to this day. At the other end Heath was virtually a spectator, but he had to be on his toes to pick out a dangerous cross from Billy Gray and a header from Les Shannon.

Burnley came more and more into the game after the interval, but even then Albion looked far superior, and in the sixtieth minute, when Allen was brought down from behind just as he was about to latch onto George Lee's centre, the home supporters thought the breakthrough had arrived as referee Frank Overton awarded the Baggies their first penalty of the season. There was a long delay, however, before the spot-kick could be taken as the Burnley defenders messed around, and when Allen finally stepped up to take the kick his direction was okay but his effort lacked power, and Thompson dived to his left to pull off a smart save, Shannon jumping for joy as it happened! Allen almost made up for his miss when a cracking drive missed the framework of the goal by a hair's breadth, and soon afterwards Lee had a shot blocked by the keeper. It was not Albion's day – their first 0-0 home draw of the season, and in fact their first goalless League encounter at The Hawthorns since 6 October 1951 (*v.* Huddersfield Town).

One newspaper reporter summed up the match thus: 'After completely dominating the first half and failing to score due to a grand Burnley defence in which goalkeeper Thompson and centre half Cummings were outstanding, and their own shortcomings in front of goal, Albion could not complain at not getting both points.' 'Albion Do It All Bar Score' stated the *Daily Mirror*.

Commenting on his penalty miss, Allen admitted: 'It wasn't the best I've ever taken nor was it the worst. The keeper guessed right and saved well. No doubt I'll get another chance against other opponents.' On this same afternoon Wolves lost 2-0 at Portsmouth, so Albion's draw took them two points clear of their Black Country rivals at the top of the Division (41-39).

Albion 0   **Burnley 0**

Ronnie Allen missed Albion's
first penalty of the season.

Club News

The chairman of the England selectors, Mr Harold Shentall, attended the Albion-Burnley game at The Hawthorns.

Albion's reserves lost 2-0 at Burnley, while the teenagers beat Sunderland 1-0 in their fourth round FA Youth Cup-tie at Roker Park, Alan Tranter scoring the vital goal in front of almost 7,000 spectators.

One of Albion's junior teams beat Oaklands Athletic 16-0 in a Birmingham Youth Committee Senior League game at Sheldon on 23 January. Terry Green scored seven times.

Albion: Heath; Rickaby, Millard; Dudley, Dugdale, Barlow; Griffin, Ryan, Allen, Nicholls, Lee.

Burnley: Thompson; Aird, Mather; Adamson, Cummings, Attwell; Gray, Stephenson, Holden, Shannon, Pilkington.

MILLERMEN CUT TO SHREDS

Date: Saturday 30 January 1954
Location: The Hawthorns
Attendance: 48,242 (receipts £36,005)

Match title: FA Cup fourth round
Referee: Mr G. Gibson (Urmston)

This was the first ever meeting between Albion and Rotherham United on a football pitch, and it was the Baggies who came out on top, winning comfortably by four clear goals on a hard, frosty pitch. As early as the second minute the 10,000 or so Rotherham fans (including a colourful but rather noisy band) and a few players shouted for a penalty when Ray Barlow and Jimmy Dugdale seemed to sandwich centre forward Ronnie Burke inside the area when going for a high ball, but referee George Gibson waved play on. Then at the other end of the field, United full-back Peter Johnson seemed to baulk Reg Ryan as goalkeeper Jack Quairney collected a high ball – but again play was waved on.

After these early incidents Albion took control, and as the game progressed it became all too easy for Vic Buckingham's men. They carved the Rotherham defence to shreds with some delightfully crisp passing football, instigated by the superb Barlow who skated over the pitch like a ballerina on ice. He was exceptional and strode through the game in masterly fashion, causing havoc in the visitors' defence every time he had the ball. His long sweeping passes, measured to perfection, dropped at the feet of his two wingers, who had the beating of the respective full-backs, Frank Griffin more often as he was much cleverer on the ball than George Lee. With the Rotherham defenders, renowned for their bustling ways and hard tackling, looking somewhat dazed and giddy, Johnny Nicholls poached two first-half goals in the fourteenth and twenty-fifth minutes. It should have been more. Nicholls' first came after a speedy raid down the Rotherham left. Allen and Ryan combined, and when the latter's low drive shot across the face of the goal, Johnny was on the spot to knock it into the net. His second was down to some more clever work by Allen. The nippy centre forward fed the final ball into his strike partner with great precision, and Nicholls pulled the trigger to send his shot goalwards, full-back Johnson making a vain attempt to keep it out.

Ray Barlow fired in two bullets at goal, and keeper Quairney tipped a crackerjack from Allen over the bar as Albion kept up the pressure. After the interval the one-way traffic continued. Rotherham simply had no answer to Albion's flowing football, and after Lee's glancing header had gone the wrong side of the post, Allen, from a standing position, got on the end of a sharp cross from Griffin to make it 3-0 on sixty-two minutes. Allen (twice), Nicholls and Lee for Albion, Burke and Wilson for Rotherham all had shots at goal before Griffin was at it again on eighty-three minutes, laying on the fourth goal for Ryan who had the easy task of finding the net from eight yards after the right-winger had bamboozled Williams and then confused both goalkeeper Quairney and left-back Johnson with some

Albion 4
Nicholls (2)
Allen
Ryan

Rotherham United 0

tricky footwork. Late on both Nicholls and Dudley had shots at goal as Rotherham soaked up an enormous amount of pressure. The visitors were outclassed, but they battled on bravely. Norman Heath had nothing to do all afternoon – he must have been freezing! Allen, who roamed all over the field covering acres of ground was Man of the Match, with Barlow a close second. It was as you were in the race for the championship as Wolves, already out of the Cup, did not have a League game.

Club News

The draw for the fifth round of the FA Cup saw Albion given another home tie, this time against Newcastle United. This was the first time since 1928/29 that the Baggies had been given three home draws in succession.

In the FA Youth Cup, Albion's youngsters were paired with Leeds United at The Hawthorns.

Stan Rickaby, Ray Barlow and Jimmy Dugdale were all selected to represent the Football League against the League of Ireland at Maine Road, Manchester on 10 February. Ronnie Allen was named as first reserve (to the forwards).

Albion manager Vic Buckingham (left) talking pre-Cup-tie tactics with Ronnie Allen (centre) and Reg Ryan, who both scored against Rotherham.

Albion: Heath; Rickaby, Millard; Dudley, Dugdale, Barlow; Griffin, Ryan, Allen, Nicholls, Lee.

Rotherham United: Quairney; Selkirk, Johnston; Marshall, Noble, Williams; Grainger, Henderson, Burke, Guest, Wilson.

BRILLIANT BARTRAM STOPS ALBION

Date: Saturday 6 February 1954
Location: The Valley
Attendance: 27,553

Match title: League
Referee: Mr R. E. Tarratt (Horsham)

Attendance: Johnny Nicholls (back injury) was absent from Albion's forward line on a foggy and very cold afternoon in south-east London, as Ray Barlow made his 250th senior appearance for the club – and once again the big man played exceptionally well in the centre of the field as his team dominated the first half, but found veteran goalkeeper Sam Bartram in superb form.

Left-winger Billy Kiernan leapt above Stan Rickaby to get the game's first header, Heath saving easily. At the other end Reg Ryan got in behind Cyril Hammond and Bartram, but couldn't connect with George Lee's high centre. A scramble inside the Charlton penalty area resulted in a free-kick on the six-yard line for the home side, and soon afterwards Ryan set up Wilf Carter, deputising for Nicholls, whose shot flew inches wide. In the seventeenth minute Kiernan hobbled off with an injured knee. This gave Albion a slight advantage, although the Addicks chased and harried every move. Stuart Leary and then Sid O'Linn had chances; likewise Ronnie Allen and Griffin at the other end, but it was Bartram who caught the eye, saving brilliantly from Ryan and then Carter. It was goalless at half-time, although the home fans could not have grumbled had Albion gone in two or three goals to the good.

Eight minutes and two more attacks after the break Albion deservedly took the lead. The ball was quickly switched from one end of the field to the other and when Barlow delivered a dangerous ball into the penalty area, Allen got in front of centre half Derek Ufton to head home in style, giving Bartram no chance of saving. Kiernan returned to the fray on the hour mark and moved to left-back, allowing Eddie Firmani to push forward, but with Ufton struggling with two damaged ankles, Charlton relied on their forwards to do the business and after some close shaves at both ends of The Valley, they eventually scrambled an equaliser through Bobby Ayre with just five minutes remaining. In the end it was a fair result to an exciting game – although deep down Albion knew they should have won on their first-half performance. Wolves beat Blackpool 4-1 at Molineux to close the gap at the top of the Division One table to just one point (42-41). Bolton Wanderers were now in third position on 37 points.

Club News

On 6 February, Albion's junior team crashed to a 9-1 defeat at the hands of the Handsworth League XI in a friendly match at Erdington.

On the same day the reserves beat Chesterfield 3-0, Elfed Evans scoring twice.

Charlton Athletic 1
Ayre

Albion 1
Allen

CHARLTON ATHLETIC v. ALBION

Above: Ronnie Allen was again on target for the Baggies.

Left: Evergreen skipper Len Millard putting a point across in the dressing room.

Charlton Athletic: Bartram; Campbell, Firmani; Hewie, Ufton, Hammond; Hurst, Ayre, Leary, O'Linn, Kiernan.
Albion: Heath; Rickaby, Millard; Dudley, Dugdale, Barlow; Griffin, Ryan, Allen, Carter, Lee.

GRAND ALBION REVIVAL AFTER SHOCK START

Date: Saturday 13 February 1954
Location: The Hawthorns
Attendance: 38,475

Match title: League
Referee: Mr A. Bond (London)

Unfortunately, owing to a recurrence of his back injury, initially suffered in the Inter-League game at Maine Road and aggravated at The Valley, coupled with a cold, Ray Barlow was missing from the Albion line-up. Billy Brookes slotted in at left half. The Yorkshire club, thirteenth in the table, had won three of their previous four League games and were in reasonably good form; so much so that they dominated the early proceedings and took a surprise two-goal lead inside fifteen minutes while attacking the Birmingham Road End. But Albion fought back superbly, got back on level terms before half-time and then took control of the game to run out convincing winners 4-2.

After George Lee had missed an open goal in Albion's first attack, Wednesday swept downfield and took the lead on two minutes. Following a pass from Jackie Sewell, the ball bounced around inside the Albion penalty area before Dennis Woodhead pounced on it to drive it low past Norman Heath from twelve yards. Almost immediately, with Albion and their supporters shell-shocked, centre forward Jack Shaw grabbed a second after Alan Finney's low cross had eluded two defenders and the goalkeeper. There was a hush of bewilderment around The Hawthorns. The Albion players, undeterred, quickly found their feet and started to play some delightful football, with Jimmy Dudley and Reg Ryan working overtime in midfield. Allen had a drive charged down by centre half Barry Butler; Griffin lashed in a cross-shot which rebounded to Ryan, whose effort was blocked and a Len Millard clearance was misheaded by Butler, only for Albion's Johnny Nicholls, standing right behind him, to shoot straight at keeper Ryalls from only six yards out. Dudley then crashed a shot against the bar and Ronnie Allen drove another effort narrowly wide. Finney, responding for Wednesday, saw his cross missed by Shaw, and Allen and Griffin got in a muddle when going for a Nicholls pass. Thankfully, the 'Poacher' quickly made amends for his early miss by crashing Ryan's superb pass high into the net past Ryalls from fifteen yards to reduce the deficit on twenty-seven minutes. With the crowd roaring them on, Albion equalised five minutes later. Dudley, who had been outstanding, moved forward before letting fly with a tremendous right-foot shot. The ball cannoned off Butler and flew into the net past Ryalls and full-back Vince Kenny on the line. Just before the break workhorse Ryan chipped a superb effort at goal, only to see the ball run down the back of the net with Nicholls waiting to pounce.

Four-and-a-half minutes into the second half Stan Rickaby scored a wonderful goal to edge Albion in front at 3-2. Collecting the ball near the halfway line, he charged forward and from fully thirty-five yards unleashed an unstoppable right-foot screamer that brushed

---

Albion 4
Nicholls, Butler (og)
Rickaby, Ryan

Sheffield Wednesday 2
Woodhead
Shaw

ALBION v. SHEFFIELD WEDNESDAY

Jimmy Dudley's strike cannons off
Butler, leaving keeper Ryalls helpless.

Ryalls' fingertips as it zoomed high into the Wednesday net. 'It was like an atomic missile – a magnificent goal' said Wednesday's manager Eric Taylor after the game. Albion boss Vic Buckingham responded by saying: 'It may not always be good tactics for full-backs to be up firing in shots, but when one goes in – we love it.' Ryan netted number four on fifty-three minutes after a cross-shot from Lee had been only partially cleared, and thereafter in it was all Albion, who should have increased their lead but for two bad misses, one by Lee and the other by Frank Griffin, who had a wonderful game, Wednesday having no answer to his tricky footwork. Ryan also headed wide from a good position, and Allen was a fraction too high with a chip shot from the edge of the area.

The local press stated: 'After their early lapses Albion went on to play some 'championship' football with Dudley and Ryan quite brilliant. As for Wednesday ... they made a game of it for at least twenty minutes.'

From Albion's point of view this match had everything – great attacking play, four fine goals and some fine individual performances – and the home crowd was delighted! Wolves went down 4-2 at Chelsea, thus enabling Albion to increase their lead at the top of the Division One table to three points (44-41) with twelve games to play.

Club News

Like the first team, Albion's reserves were 2-0 down after fifteen minutes at Hillsborough but could only score one in reply and slipped to their fourteenth defeat of the season.

The club announced that if the fifth round FA Cup-tie with Newcastle United (next Saturday) should end in a draw, the replay would take place at St James' Park on Wednesday 24 February, kick-off 2.45 p.m.

Albion: Heath; Rickaby, Millard; Dudley, Dugdale, Brookes; Griffin, Ryan, Allen, Nicholls, Lee.

Sheffield Wednesday: Ryalls; Kenny, Seemly; McAnearney, Butler, Davies; Finney, Quixall, Shaw, Sewell, Woodhead.

ALLEN IS ALBION'S HAT-TRICK HERO

Date: Saturday 20 February 1954
Location: The Hawthorns
Attendance: 61,088 (receipts £37,470)

Match title: FA Cup fifth round
Referee: Mr B.M. Griffiths (Newport)

Around 25,000 Newcastle supporters made the 220-mile journey from the north-east for this eagerly awaited Cup-tie. Two-thirds of them got in; the other 7,500, along with almost 8,000 disappointed Albion fans, were locked out, yet remained near the ground to soak up the tremendous atmosphere. The 61,000-plus crowd, the biggest at The Hawthorns for sixteen years saw a rip-roaring encounter.

Albion, at full strength, and choosing to play in red shirts and white shorts, while the Geordies donned white shirts and black shorts, performed superbly during the first half when they scored twice. United hit back strongly and reduced the deficit to one before Allen netted a screamer to complete his hat-trick. After a second Newcastle goal, Albion had to withstand a last-ditch charge from the Cup favourites, but ran out deserved winners after a memorable contest.

Albion went in front as early as the fifth minute. Reg Ryan got in a low drive from just outside the area, and as the ball came back Allen pounced to drill an unstoppable left-foot shot into the net past the diving Ronnie Simpson as full-back Bobby Cowell came in far too late with his challenge. With Albion well in control, George Lee, Ray Barlow and then Frank Griffin all had efforts saved, and then on twenty-three minutes, the lead was doubled. A move inspired by the long-striding Barlow was almost finished off by Johnny Nicholls – but his effort came back off the crossbar and Allen, who had raced fully twenty yards to keep up with the play, tucked away the rebound. Simpson then made a flying save from a Jimmy Dudley piledriver while at the other end of the field, Norman Heath, who had been a spectator, had to be on his toes to push a Billy Foulkes shot round the post. Just before the interval Allen had a goal disallowed and saw another shot well saved by Simpson. The Newcastle keeper also parried a smart drive from Lee.

The visitors started the second half with the song *Blaydon Races* ringing round the ground, as their loyal supporters urged them on. They responded well; Jackie Milburn sent a header over the top and had another shot saved by Heath, who also did well to keep out efforts from Ivor Broadis and Jackie Scoular. On sixty-four minutes the latter's free-kick was pumped deep into the Albion penalty area. Heath, Milburn and Broadis all went for the ball as it was punched out by the keeper, so it fell invitingly for Bobby Mitchell who drove it high into the net with his left foot – 2-1. Two more United attacks followed but both were scuppered by determined tackles from first Stan Rickaby and then by Dudley. On seventy-two minutes Albion won a corner on the left. Lee drilled the ball across waist-high for Allen, facing the flag, who caught it on the volley to send it whizzing past Simpson, who dived into thin air. In fact,

Albion 3	Newcastle United 2
Allen (3)	Mitchell
	Milburn

ALBION v. NEWCASTLE UNITED

Ronnie Allen's effort is turned
aside by the agile Simpson.

the ball almost took a defender's head off as he jumped in vain on the line. A quite brilliant goal – one of Allen's finest and without doubt one of the best ever seen at The Hawthorns.

Griffin had some back luck soon afterwards; Nicholls had two one-on-one chances after that. He missed them both, hitting the post with his second effort, and then helped out at the back as Albion had to endure a late Newcastle onslaught following an eighty-sixth minute goal from Milburn, who deflected Foulkes' low cross wide of Heath. A great occasion, great game, a great goal (Allen's third) and great win.

Alf McMichael, the Newcastle full-back, said afterwards: 'A great match. But Albion, I think, were just the better side ... Aye, just the better side.' This is what United's keeper Ronnie Simpson said about Allen's second and last goals: 'Nicholls sent in a great shot. I couldn't even get my fingers to the ball. It thudded against the crossbar and the next thing I knew Ronnie had tapped it into the net. That volley was magnificent ... I've never seen one hit so sweetly. I hadn't a dog's chance of saving it.'

Wolves were in League action against Sheffield United, and they took advantage by winning 6-1 to close the gap at the top to just one point (44-43), Albion had a game in hand.

Club News

Albion were again drawn at home in the FA Cup, and this time their sixth round opponents on 13 March would be Tottenham Hotspur.

Allen's hat-trick against Newcastle was his sixth for Albion. It was also the first time an Albion player had netted a Cup treble in five years – Dave Walsh being the last against Chelsea in 1949.

On 20 February Albion's junior team beat Handsworth All Stars 12-2 in a Birmingham Youth Committee League game.

Albion: Heath; Rickaby, Millard; Dudley, Dugdale, Barlow; Griffin, Ryan, Allen, Nicholls, Lee.

Newcastle United: Simpson; Cowell, McMichael; Scoular, Brennan, Stokoe; Foulkes, Broadis, Milburn, Hannah, Mitchell.

ALLEN'S 29TH GOAL IS NOT QUITE ENOUGH

Date: Wednesday 24 February 1954   **Match title:** League
Location: Ayresome Park   **Referee:** Mr J.H. Clough (Bolton)
Attendance: 17,144

Unchanged from that terrific Cup win over Newcastle, Albion travelled to Teesside to play their rearranged League game with Middlesbrough knowing that a victory would take them three points clear of their Black Country rivals Wolves.

In front of what was to be the lowest attendance of the season (home and away) Albion had to work hard to gain a point against a relegation-threatened side that competed with great honesty and endeavour throughout the ninety minutes, just like they had done at The Hawthorns earlier in the season.

The match turned out to be an intriguing contest between skill and speed on the part of Albion and grit and hard-tackling from Middlesbrough, for whom Wilf Mannion was once again a star performer.

In a very competitive first half, Stan Rickaby, playing against his former club, got in the first real tackle to deny Jimmy Hartnett, and then Lindy Delaphena's effort went three yards wide.

Johnny Nicholls, Ronnie Allen, Ryan and Jimmy Dudley all had decent shots at goal for Albion, but generally speaking the defences remained on top. That is until the fifty-sixth minute, when Allen, escaping from his marker (Dickie Robinson) nipped in to send a smart header past Rolando Ugolini to score his 100th senior goal for Albion in a total of 175 games.

It was his twenty-ninth strike of the season, and came about following a fine build-up down the left from where Ryan crossed to Griffin, whose attempt on goal came to Allen who didn't miss from close range.

Inspired by Mannion, Boro hit back strongly, and in the sixty-third minute Jimmy Dugdale was penalised for a late tackle (from behind) on centre forward Bill Edwards, allowing Delaphena to step up and beat Heath from the penalty spot for the equaliser. Dugdale, never at ease against Edwards, committed another foul on the striker on seventy minutes, but this time Delaphena's free-kick from fully twenty yards flew over the bar.

Barlow, with a thumping shot from twenty-five yards, Allen, who was kept fairly quiet for most of the game by Robinson, Nicholls and Griffin for Albion, and both Edwards and Joe Rayment for Boro all went close before referee Clough ended the contest with honours even after four minutes of injury time had been added. With this draw at Ayresome Park Albion extended their lead over Wolves at the top of the table to two points (45-43) with eleven games remaining.

Middlesbrough 1   **Albion 1**
    Delaphena (pen)   Allen

Club News

Goalkeeper Norman Heath received a severe groin strain against Middlesbrough and was under intense treatment for two days before being declared unfit to face Huddersfield Town at Leeds Road. This ended a run of thirty-four consecutive League and Cup appearances for Albion.

Above: Ray Barlow went close with a 25-yard drive.

Right: Jimmy Dugdale conceded a penalty.

Middlesbrough: Ugolini; Stonehouse, Corbett; Bell, Robinson, Dicks; Rayment, Mannion, Edwards, Delaphena, Hartnett.

Albion: Heath; Rickaby, Millard; Dudley, Dugdale, Barlow; Griffin, Ryan, Allen, Nicholls, Lee.

A SHOW OF YORKSHIRE GRIT FROM ALBION

Date: Saturday 27 February 1954
Location: Leeds Road
Attendance: 48,237

Match title: League
Referee: Mr J. Houston (Lytham St Anne's)

Jimmy Sanders was brought into the team (in place of Heath) for his first senior outing of the season and he played really well (handling the ball competently and taking every cross) against an attack-minded Huddersfield Town side who, prior to this match, had netted fifty-six goals, were lying third in the table and were unbeaten at home. Albion – totally committed from the first to the last whistle, although lacking a little of their usual polish – deserved their win and duly ended the Terriers' excellent record at Leeds Road, their previous defeat in front of their own supporters having been suffered back in February 1953 (twenty-three matches ago). It was also the Baggies' fifth double of the season.

An unfortunate aggravated injury to rugged centre half Don McEvoy, who left the field in the first half, certainly disrupted Huddersfield's plan of action, but Albion always had the upper hand and were generally the better side despite some tenacious, enterprising and strong forward play by the home side.

Surprisingly, having had six efforts on goal during the first forty-five minutes (two of them saved magnificently by keeper Harry Mills), Albion had to wait until the forty-eighth minute before taking the lead, Reg Ryan flying in to head home a beautifully delivered left-wing corner taken by George Lee. Home keeper Mills, always busy, then pulled off a string of fine saves after that, before Johnny Nicholls swooped onto Ronnie Allen's deft pass to make it 2-0 on eighty-two minutes. Huddersfield continued to fight for every ball, and Albion had to defend in numbers to keep their fortress intact. Every member of Vic Buckingham's team pulled his weight, and victory was achieved the hard way, one reporter describing it as 'Efficient, workmanlike and very professional.' The Albion programme (for the home game with Sheffield United a week later) stated: 'Huddersfield did not intend to surrender their valuable home record without a determined struggle. They attacked with considerable fire and no little skill.'

Newcastle United did Albion a huge favour by beating Wolves 3-2 at St James' Park, and as a result the points gap at the top of the Division was stretched to four (47-43) and now there were just ten games remaining.

Club News

On 3 March England 'B' were held to a 1-1 draw by Scotland 'B' at Roker Park, Sunderland. Three Albion players took part in the match: Ronnie Allen and Jimmy Dugdale (England) *v.* Jimmy Dudley (Scotland).

Huddersfield Town 0

Albion 2
Ryan
Nicholls

HUDDERSFIELD TOWN v. ALBION

A crowd of over 5,500 saw Albion's youngsters beat Leeds United 3-1 (after extra time) in their fifth round FA Youth Cup-tie on Saturday 27 February. Brian Whitehouse scored twice.

This completed a double for Albion over Leeds as the reserves won a Central League game 3-2 at The Hawthorns three days earlier. This was followed up with a 2-0 home win over Everton, Wilf Carter scoring two excellent goals.

Alas, Albion's interest in the Staffordshire Senior Cup ended when Wolves beat them 1-0 at Molineux in the second round.

Jimmy Sanders (goalkeeper) and Len Millard played in the League side for the first time this season at Huddersfield, and both performed well in a competent 2-0 victory.

Huddersfield Town: Mills; Staniforth, Kelly; McGarry, McEvoy, Watson; Burrell, Freer, Glazzard, Cavanagh, Metcalf.

Albion: Sanders; Rickaby, Millard; Dudley, Dugdale, Barlow; Griffin, Ryan, Allen, Nicholls, Lee.

ALBION CUT BACK BY SHARP BLADES

Date: Saturday 6 March 1954
Location: The Hawthorns
Attendance: 37,650

Match title: League
Referee: Mr R. Haworth (Blackburn)

Norman Heath was still an absentee as Albion entertained a tough, resilient Sheffield United side at The Hawthorns a week before their FA Cup quarter-final clash with Spurs. Albion, attacking the Birmingham Road goal with a strong wind behind them, made the early running and twice came close to scoring before the Blades sharpened up and tested Jimmy Sanders. A flying header from Ronnie Allen went wide; a Johnny Nicholls' shot grazed the bar and then the same player hit it as United were pressed back. Reg Ryan then struck a post while a Nicholls sent a header straight at goalkeeper Ted Burgin. Jimmy Hagan, later to manage Albion, created an opening for Alf Ringstead and Peter Wragg's hopeful 25-yard shot was easily claimed by the Albion keeper. United, third from bottom, looked dangerous on the break and Hagan went close to putting the visitors ahead. Ringstead did likewise with a snap shot from just outside the penalty area. With both their wingers driving forward, Albion certainly had more of the game during the first half but they had to wait until a minute before the break before taking the lead. Allen gathered Jimmy Dudley's ground pass wide on the right, and after adroitly getting himself into position, he was able to deliver the perfect cross for Nicholls to rise majestically and head firmly past Burgin's outstretched right arm.

Shortly after the break George Lee almost made it 2-0 but was off-target, while at the other end of the field Jack Cross got the better of Jimmy Dugdale but his shot lacked direction. In the fiftieth minute Albion scored their second goal. Allen again wandered out to the right where he collected Nicholls' pass and centred quickly. Coming under pressure from Lee, United's keeper Burgin caught the ball but then dropped it. The winger was first to react and swept the ball into the net with Nicholls, as usual, close at hand, just in case! Soon afterwards the United woodwork was rattled as Albion went in search of a third goal. The Blades, dogged and as combative as ever – and with the wind still pretty strong and in their favour – reduced the deficit on the hour mark. A left-sided free-kick by Graham Shaw found Hagan inside the Albion penalty area. He crashed a shot against the bar and as the ball dropped down, Wragg pounced to hit the rebound high past Heath and into the net via the underside of the crossbar. With Albion on the back foot, United pressed forward and after a close shave, the visitors equalised on seventy-one minutes, and once again it was Wragg who found the net. Hagan's throw-in bypassed Stan Rickaby out on the right, and when the ball was whipped in, Cross nodded it forward for Wragg to spurt in between defenders to head wide of Heath's left hand. This set the Baggies thinking. They were hard-pressed for a time but got over the crisis, drove forward

Albion 2
Nicholls
Lee

Sheffield United 2
Wragg (2)

Ronnie Allen came so close to opening the scoring with this diving header.

and Lee had a shot cleared off the line by Johnson, while Burgin made a sensational save from Paddy Ryan's well-directed header. Late on Allen almost won it with a well-struck drive that Joe Shaw somehow got a foot to and deflected out for a corner.

One tabloid reporter explained: 'It was a point lost by Albion – but these sort of days are bound to occur – and better this week than next!' With Wolves going down to a 1-0 defeat away to Manchester United, the draw sent Albion three points clear once again at the head of the table (48-45). Huddersfield Town (forty-one points) were still in there with a shout.

Club News

On Monday 8 March, former Albion goalkeeper Joe Reader died in Hallam Hospital, West Bromwich, at the age of eighty-eight. He made 370 senior League and Cup appearances for the club between 1885 and 1901, gained an FA Cup winner's medal and was capped once by England.

Albion's Second XI lost 1-0 to Wolves at Molineux; the Handsworth League side beat 904 RASC Coy 9-1 and the 'A' team defeated Moor Green 3-0 in the Tillotson Cup.

It was announced that should Albion's sixth round Cup-tie end in a draw, the replay would take place at White Hart Lane on Wednesday 17 March, kick-off 2.30 p.m.

Albion: Sanders; Rickaby, Millard; Dudley, Dugdale, Barlow; Griffin, Ryan, Allen, Nicholls, Lee.
Sheffield United: Burgin; Johnson, G. Shaw; J. Shaw, Coldwell, Rawson; Ringstead, Hagan, Cross, Wragg, McNabb.

A CLASSIC SHOW FROM VIC'S MEN

Date: Saturday 13 March 1954
Location: The Hawthorns
Attendance: 51,049 (receipts: £36,554)

Match title: FA Cup sixth round
Referee: Mr A.E. Ellis (Halifax)

Albion were back to full strength for this eagerly-awaited Cup encounter with Spurs, beaten semi-finalists in 1953. Losing the toss, Albion attacked the Birmingham Road goal in the first half and early on Ronnie Allen's shot was smothered at the second attempt by keeper Ted Ditchburn, with Johnny Nicholls ready to pounce. Ditchburn was continually in action as Albion's five-man attack stormed forward. He saved well from Reg Ryan and then George Lee, but was eventually beaten by Nicholls on seventeen minutes. Allen fed his strike-partner with a decisive through ball, and as the keeper left his line, Nicholls clipped a sweet left-footed shot into the net. Ditchburn then clawed a teasing Griffin cross away from Ryan, while at the other end Norman Heath got both fists to the ball to punch away a swinging cross from George Robb. On the stroke of half-time Len Duquemin could have equalised but his weak effort dribbled wide.

In the forty-ninth minute Albion doubled their lead. They won a free-kick on the edge of the 'D'. Ronnie Allen normally had a crack but this time Ray Barlow took over the mantle and his wonderful left-footer flew into the net via Ditchburn's right hand after going straight through a badly-organised defensive wall. Albion were teasing and tormenting Spurs at this stage in the proceedings, and a brilliant three-man move involving Allen, Lee and Nicholls ended with the latter diving forward in front of Bill Nicholson to head home the winger's perfectly flighted cross for his side's third goal in the sixty-seventh minute, the ball entering the net via Ditchburn's left-hand upright. Only Robb, Lee's counterpart, posed any threat to a dominant back line, and one of his efforts grazed the bar while another was saved by the alert and well-positioned Heath.

When Jimmy Dugdale had to go off to have four stitched inserted in a nasty head wound following a seventy-seventh minute clash with Clarke, Barlow took over at centre half and his first task was to stop Duquemin from bursting through the middle. He then produced a splendid tackle to halt Baily. Ditchburn was in action late on, saving a piledriver from Allen and a right-footed shot from Nicholls who was seeking his hat-trick. As Albion kept on going to the last, Nicholls almost caught the keeper out with a deceiving centre and Ryan shot wide. Albion won at a canter. They were in their fourteenth FA Cup semi-final. The Spurs manager Arthur Rowe was too ill to attend the game but he sent a letter to his opposite number, Vic Buckingham, which read: 'It is not a pleasure to be beaten by you – but at least it is no disgrace.'

Charles Richards in the *Daily Mail* wrote: 'Albion 'coasted' into their 14th semi-final...they were always superior and Spurs were played out of the picture.' Rex Bellamy

---

Albion 3
Barlow
Nicholls (2)

Tottenham Hotspur 0

(*Daily Express*) stated: 'Albion smashed Spurs so easily, so gently.' Scottie Hall of the *Post* thought 'It's Albion for the double on this form.' Frank Butler (*News of the World*) agreed with Hall, and added: 'There can be little dispute that Albion are the finest team in the country. They over-ran Spurs.' Albion were now 5-4 clear favourites with bookmaker William Hill to win the Cup. Preston North End were quoted at 3-1, Bolton Wanderers 4-1 and Sheffield Wednesday 10-1.

Wolves were without a game and so there was no change at the top of the Division One table.

Club News

The draw for the semi-finals of the FA Cup took place on Monday lunchtime (15 March) and Albion were paired with Staffordshire rivals Port Vale, runaway leaders of the Third Division (North) at Villa Park while Sheffield Wednesday would take on Preston North End in a Roses battle at Maine Road – both ties taking place on Saturday 27 March, kick-off 3.00 p.m.

Three players – Frank Griffin (knee), Stan Rickaby (thigh) and Johnny Nicholls (back) – all reported to club physiotherapist Fred Pedley for treatment prior to the midweek trip to Stamford Bridge. They were declared fit to play on the morning of the game.

Ray Barlow's wonderful free-kick flies past Spurs keeper Ted Ditchburn to put Albion 2-0 ahead.

Albion: Heath; Rickaby, Millard; Dudley, Dugdale, Barlow; Griffin, Ryan, Allen, Nicholls, Lee.

Tottenham Hotspur: Ditchburn; Ramsey, Willis; Nicholson, Clarke, Burgess; Walters, Bennett, Duquemin, Baily, Robb.

ALBION BLOWN AWAY AT THE BRIDGE

Date: Wednesday 17 March 1954
Location: Stamford Bridge
Attendance: 46,089

Match title: League
Referee: Mr F.L. Overton (Derby)

Unchanged and playing in red shirts and white shorts, Albion – unbeaten in a club record fourteen League and Cup games – came under pressure from the start as Chelsea started off like a Formula One racing driver at the commencement of a Grand Prix. They tore at the Baggies' defence and had three shots at goal inside the first two minutes. Then keeper Norman Heath had to race off his line and kick the ball away as Roy Bentley challenged. Albion eventually came out of their shell, and Reg Ryan sent in two shots himself. One struck the crossbar, the other an upright. Nothing really went right for the Irishman on St Patrick's Day!

On eight minutes the Blues went ahead, Derek Saunders' long-range effort squeezing past everybody and entering the net via an upright. Just four minutes later it was 2-0 to the Londoners after a brilliant run by Roy Bentley gave John McNichol an easy tap in from point-blank range. Albion were desperately unlucky when two fierce drives by Reg Ryan struck the woodwork – the first came down off the underside of the crossbar; the second rebounded from an upright. In the thirtieth minute Chelsea netted a lucky third goal when Les Stubbs was on hand to knock in Bentley's low cross. The centre forward's initial shot rebounded straight back to him, and with Albion's defence in a tangle, the England international picked out his team-mate. Albion conceded again three minutes later when Jim Lewis scored following a smart move involving Eric Parsons, Stubbs and Bentley, the latter providing the final pass.

Albion, shell-shocked at having given away four goals in a game for the first time since the end of October, and, in fact, at having conceded four in the opening half of a game for the first time since February 1937 (at Stoke), hit back strongly in the second half, and Stan Willemse, the Chelsea full-back, cleared Ronnie Allen's header off the line. The same defender then scrambled the ball away from the danger-zone as Nicholls charged in, and soon afterwards both Allen and Ryan fired wide. For all their efforts, the Chelsea barrier could not be broken down. Then, to add salt to Albion's already deep wound, Bentley, who had given Jimmy Dugdale plenty of problems all afternoon, crowned a fine display by making it 5-0 in the eightieth minute with a fine opportunist effort – and the same player almost netted again soon afterwards but was denied by a fine one-handed save from Heath. To their credit Albion kept on trying to play football. They regularly had four men in attack and realistically should have had at least three goals for their commitment. But it was not to be and in the end they were on the receiving end of a 5-0 drubbing, their heaviest defeat of the season. Indeed, it was their first nap-hand reverse since losing by the same score at Burnley on 3 January 1953.

Chelsea 5
    Saunders, McNichol
    Stubbs, Lewis
    Bentley

Albion 0

The reporter in the *Birmingham Post* stated: 'It was not a good day for Barlow, who lost the ball too frequently in midfield. Each time, in a flash, it was whipped forward and another Chelsea attack was in motion.' Manager Vic Buckingham said: 'There wasn't too much to choose between the two sides. Our three 'woodwork shots' came out and theirs went in – that tells its own story. Our bad luck began when Chelsea decided to play so inspired a game.' Wolves didn't have a game in midweek and therefore Albion had now played one match more than their rivals (34 to 33) but still led Division One by three points.

Club News

It was announced that Albion's FA Cup semi-final clash with Port Vale would be all-ticket affair with a limit of 70,000. Both teams could claim up to 30,000 tickets each. Albion asked for their full allocation (and a few more) and would sell them at The Hawthorns on Sunday 21 March, as follows: for the terracing – 2/6 (12½p) and 2s (10p) and for seats – 6s (30p).

Albion keeper Norman Heath played very well at Stamford Bridge despite conceding five goals.

Chelsea: Robertson; Harris, Willemse; Armstrong, Greenwood, D. Saunders; Parsons, McNichol, Bentley, Stubbs, Lewis.

Albion: Heath; Rickaby, Millard; Dudley, Dugdale, Barlow; Griffin, Ryan, Allen, Nicholls, Lee.

SWEET REVENGE FOR BELOW-PAR ALBION

Date: Saturday 20 March 1954
Location: The Hawthorns
Attendance: 53,210

Match title: League
Referee: Mr K.A. Collinge (Sale)

Blackpool had defeated Albion 4-1 at Bloomfield Road earlier in the season yet, as holders of the trophy, had also been knocked out of the FA Cup by Albion's semi-final opponents Port Vale. Stan Rickaby, injured in the heavy defeat at Chelsea, was replaced at right-back by Stuart Williams. The Seasiders were missing Stan Mortensen, and were on an unbeaten run of five matches. Albion's biggest home League crowd of the season witnessed a moderate match in which both defences were strong and unyielding. Few clear-cut chances were created, although Albion did have far more possession than Blackpool, and in the end just about deserved to win despite producing a rather disappointing performance. In truth, Albion had the upper hand over their challengers in two areas; down the left flank where Len Millard, Ray Barlow and George Lee played exceptionally well, and at centre half where Jimmy Dugdale was brilliant, winning virtually everything in the air. Norman Heath was also outstanding in goal.

After George Farm had safely gathered a long-range shot from Ronnie Allen, Blackpool, against the run of play, took the lead on five minutes when Scotsman Jackie Mudie netted after a right-wing move involving two Englishmen, Ernie Taylor, the smallest player on the pitch, and his right-wing partner Stanley Matthews. It was the latter's cross, missed by Dugdale, that set Mudie up for the kill. Blackpool held out as Albion went in search of an equaliser. Indeed, the Seasiders frequently passed back to keeper George Farm from afar Albion perhaps at times played too intricately in the centre of the field, choosing to deliver one pass too many, but eventually they did equalise on thirty-eight minutes when Jimmy Dudley's low pass into the penalty area was smartly back-heeled by Reg Ryan to Allen who, finding himself in space behind Harry Johnson, netted with a well-taken shot.

Albion pressed hard in the second half, and with the watery sun shining brightly, Farm had to push Griffin's teasing right-wing cross over the bar. Twice the visitors counter-attacked and the brilliance of Heath prevented the Seasiders from regaining the lead. The in-form Albion keeper pulled off two superlative saves from Mudie and Drurie to keep his side on level terms. Albion hit back strongly and after Nicholls had missed a real sitter from no less than five yards, in the sixty-ninth minute Ryan put the Baggies in front. Allen's cross was pushed out by Farm; Frank Griffin seized the loose ball and returned it quickly into the danger-zone where Ryan timed his jump to head home from eight yards. There were nervous moments late in the game for Albion when first South African-born winger Bill Perry charged through unchallenged but somehow lobbed the ball wide, and

Albion 2	Blackpool 1
Allen	Scorers
Ryan	

Right: Stuart Williams, replacing Stan Rickaby, did well to contain Bill Perry. *Far right:* Reg Ryan scored Albion's match-winner

then Taylor, in the very last minute, missed the goal with only Heath in front of him. There was no harder worker on the pitch than match-winner Ryan.

It was a good result for Albion – and the perfect build-up for what they knew was going to be one mightily tough battle against the team with the meanest defence in the whole country, Port Vale, in the Cup semi-final at Villa Park. Wolves won 1-0 at Preston and so it was still Albion ahead in the championship stakes, leading their Black Country neighbours by 50 points to 48 after both clubs had played thirty-five games. On 24 March, Wolves were held to a 1-1 draw at Molineux by Bolton, and so the deficit was cut to one point, leaving Albion with a game in hand (away at Sunderland).

Club News

Albion reported that they had sold 33,354 tickets for their semi-final showdown with Port Vale at Villa Park. If the game ended level then the replay would take place at The Victoria Ground, Stoke, on Wednesday 31 March, thus meaning that Albion's trip to Sunderland would be postponed.

Only one player – Stan Rickaby – was in for treatment after the Blackpool game, and come Thursday afternoon, he was reported fit to take on the Vale at Villa Park.

Albion's Second XI lost 2-1 at home to Manchester City while John Moore scored five times as the juniors beat Tower United 8-0 at Jaffray Road in a Birmingham Youth Committee League game.

Albion: Heath; S. Williams, Millard; Dudley, Dugdale, Barlow; Griffin, Ryan, Allen, Nicholls, Lee.
Blackpool: Farm; Greatrix, Wright; Fenton, Johnston, Kelly; Matthews, Taylor, Mudie, Drurie, Perry.

ALBION WIN A BRUISING ENCOUNTER

Date: to go here   **Match title:** FA Cup semi-final
Location: Villa Park   **Referee:** Mr H. Webb (Leeds)
Attendance: 68,221 (record receipts of £20,086 12s)

Prior to this game Albion – the highest scorers in the whole of the Football League – had spent quite some time discussing tactics on how to break down the best defence in the country – Vale having conceded just seventeen goals in their forty-one competitive matches. Isaiah Birks, a 70-year-old Vale supporter, travelled from Trenton, New Jersey, USA, specifically for the occasion.

Ex-Vale player Ronnie Allen had the first shot at goal, Ray King easily collecting the ball in his midriff. But Vale, defending deeply on a man for man basis, clamped down quickly on Albion's constructive play, some of their tackles causing grimaces on the faces of their victims, George Lee being a particular target! Albion, looking over-anxious at times, knew they would have to summon every ounce of skill and determination they could muster to wreck the growing assurance of the Valiants, a team brimming in belief and self-confidence as the minutes ticked by. After two near misses, one at each end of the field, Vale struck a hammer blow on thirty-nine minutes. With Albion wrestling to pull themselves together, outside right Colin Askey crossed an awkward ball deep into the heart of the Baggies' goalmouth, which the leaping figure of Norman Heath could only punch away. Dickie Cunliffe collected the ball out left and swung it back into the centre. It evaded both attackers and defenders before Vale's inside right Albert Leake pounced to scramble it home.

Albion trooped off at half-time with their chins on their kneecaps, but the break acted as a safety valve and when they reappeared for the start of the second period, they pushed Vale back deep into their own half with a series of penetrating attacks. Looking more composed, Albion fought back and they drew level with a goal out of the blue from Jimmy Dudley.

Charles Harold of the *Sports Argus* described it thus: 'The equaliser came in the 62nd minute and its execution was the surprising feature of the score. Dudley's flighted centre hung like a magnet as it dropped towards the Vale goal, pulling the twin striking power of Allen and Nicholls in at a colossal pace. As the Albion duo raced into the six-yard box Vale keeper King was so distracted that he misjudged the flight of the ball and it passed untouched into the net by the far post.'

Albion continued to come up against Vale's brick-wall defence, and much of their effort was relative to the impact of a ping-pong ball bouncing against a plate glass window. Suddenly the clouds of anxiety parted and Albion boomed in with one broadside after another. Allen cracked in two piledrivers, both saved by King, and Nicholls headed over as Vale came under severe pressure. Wingers Frank Griffin and Lee began to find cracks in the Vale defence as they jinked their way down the flanks, and when Lee was upended for the

Albion 2	Port Vale 1
Dudley	Leake
Allen (pen)	

Ronnie Allen's well-struck penalty
takes Albion to Wembley.

umpteenth time, referee Webb pointed to the penalty spot, although afterwards film-footage showed that the offence had actually been committed a foot outside the box. Just reward, however, for Albion, as two earlier fouls (on Allen and Lee) had both been committed inside the area but had gone unpunished. Allen placed the ball on the spot for one of the most critical and soul-searching moments of his career. He kept his cool and buried his shot low past the keeper's right hand and into the bottom corner of the net. Allen had cemented a lifelong memory – for he had dreamed, many years earlier, that he would score the winning goal (for Albion) in a Cup semi-final.

A tremendous roar went up – Albion were on their way to Wembley – and although Vale tried to fight back, Leake having a goal disallowed for offside, they had lost the willpower and during the final stages of the game it was all Albion with Allen, Nicholls and Griffin all going close to adding to the score.

After the game Albion's keeper Norman Heath told his counterpart, Ray King: 'You had all the bad luck', while Cheadle said to Allen 'Go and win the Cup for Staffordshire.'

Wolves lost 4-2 at home to lowly Middlesbrough, and so failed to close the gap behind Albion who still led the First Division table by 50 points to 48 with a game in hand.

Club News
Stan Rickaby (thigh injury), Len Millard (jarred knee) and Frank Griffin (bruised knee and sprained ankle) – were all ruled out of Albion's next game, away to relegation-threatened Sunderland.

Meanwhile Albion's 'Terrible Twins' – Ronnie Allen and Johnny Nicholls – were called up into the England team for the international with Scotland at Hampden Park, and they would miss the game at Roker Park and the vital League tussle with Wolves at The Hawthorns the next Saturday.

Albion: Heath; Rickaby, Millard; Dudley, Dugdale, Barlow; Griffin, Ryan, Allen, Nicholls, Lee.
Port Vale: King; Turner, Potts; Mullard, Cheadle, Sproson; Askey, Leake, Hayward, Tomlinson, Cunliffe.

LATE STRIKE DENIES BATTLING BAGGIES

Date: Wednesday 31 March 1954
Location: Roker Park
Attendance: 48,060

Match title: League
Referee: Mr J. McCann (Preston)

Vic Buckingham was forced to make five changes to the team that had won through to Wembley – Joe Kennedy and Stuart Williams took over the two full-back positions, Grenville Jones (making his Football League debut) replaced Griffin and the veteran Freddie Cox and young Wilf Carter deputised for Allen and Nicholls who were away on international duty. In the very first minute Kennedy was injured when trying to stop Billy Elliott, and after treatment he hobbled out to the right wing where he remained for the rest of the game. Undaunted, Albion attacked strongly and came close to opening the scoring on two occasions.

Ted Purdon and Len Shackleton opened up Albion's defence but the latter shot wide. Then left-winger Billy Elliott cut in but his cross was too high for everybody and went out for a throw-in on the far side of the pitch. Another Purdon effort went wide and Jack Chisholm headed straight at Heath, while at the other end Reg Ryan and Wilf Carter both got in shots which were easily collected by Jimmy Cowan. Then, out of the blue, as so often happens, Sunderland edged in front on thirty-two minutes when Elliott netted after a lucky ricochet and two misplaced passes!

Four minutes later, disaster struck Albion as goalkeeper Norman Heath dived at the feet of Purdon, the former Birmingham City centre forward, badly jarring his spine. He was taken off on a stretcher and rushed to hospital, by which time paralysis had set in. Ray Barlow took over the green jersey and Reg Ryan moved back to wing half as Albion, now down to nine fit men, set about chasing an equaliser. They came mighty close on a couple of occasions, first through Carter and then winger Grenville Jones, but Sunderland's defence held firm until the fifty-seventh minute when Freddie Cox, taking a short forward pass, slammed the ball past Cowan from twelve yards.

Soon afterwards it went from bad to worse for Albion when Lee was crocked. He carried on after treatment but was no more than a passenger on his own wing. At this point Albion came under considerable pressure and although Barlow pulled off two brilliant saves, four minutes from time Purdon snatched a dramatic winner for the home side, scoring in a goalmouth scramble after first Williams and then Dugdale had thought they had cleared Elliott's left-wing cross. Right on time Cox hit the side-netting when a ball across the face of the goal might have proved more beneficial. Albion didn't deserve to lose, but more worrying now was the lengthy injury list that was causing some concern back at The Hawthorns. There was no change at the top: Albion 50 points, Wolves 48 with six matches left to play. With so many injury worries, the big question everyone was asking was could Albion hold on?

Sunderland 2
Elliott
Purdon

Albion 1
Cox

Club News

On 31 March, Albion's youngsters met Manchester United (the up-and-coming Busby Babes) in the first leg of the FA Youth Cup semi-final at The Hawthorns. A crowd of over 8,000 saw the Reds win 3-1, thus making the return leg at Old Trafford a tough proposition for the Baggies.

Teenager John Moore scored five goals as Albion's junior team beat Saltley Highfield 10-2 in a Birmingham Youth Committee League game at Erdington.

Above: Wilf Carter deputised for Johnny Nicholls. *Right:* Grenville Jones made his debut at Roker Park.

Sunderland: Cowan; Stelling, Hedley; Anderson, Aitken, A. Wright; T. Wright, Shackleton, Purdon, Chisholm, Elliott.

Albion: Heath; Kennedy, S. Williams; Dudley, Dugdale, Barlow; Jones, Ryan, Cox, Carter, Lee.

ALBION BITTEN BY HUNGRY WOLVES, AGAIN!

Date: Saturday 3 April 1954
Location: The Hawthorns
Attendance: 49,884

Match title: League
Referee: Mr F. Cowen (Manchester)

A crowd of 60,000 was anticipated for this crucial match but Wolves brought with them under 10,000 supporters and consequently the attendance was surprisingly low for such an important game. Albion made seven changes, three of them positional, while Wolves were without Billy Wright and Jimmy Mullen, both on England international duty with Allen and Nicholls in Glasgow. Reg Cutler was brought in on Albion's left-wing for only his fourth League outing in two years.

Most national scribes tipped Wolves to win this battle of the giants, owing to Albion's depleted team – and they were right. Albion battled hard and long and probably deserved a share of the points but Roy Swinbourne grabbed the all-important goal and put the championship race back into the melting pot. It turned out to be a dour, scrappy local derby, played on a rather uneven pitch with a strong, tantalising breeze occasionally causing problems. It lacked overall method and finesse, yet the action was cut and thrust, parry and riposte with tempers fraying from time to time. Wolves' skipper for the day, Bill Shorthouse, in a robust and miserly mood, stopped Barlow in the eighth minute with a rock-solid challenge. The Albion left half, playing as an emergency centre forward, was badly injured and was a limping passenger thereafter. It was a crucial blow, and soon afterwards Reg Ryan took a crack on the ankle and for a while he too hobbled around in pain. Referee Cowen spoke to Shorthouse and Roy Pritchard for two reckless tackles, and then Wilf Carter sent a free-kick inches wide. Wolves, using the 'long boot' to good effect, pinned Albion back for a good ten minutes, but Jimmy Sanders was as safe as houses behind his defence.

After half-time Wolves pushed forward more positively and in the fifty-eighth minute struck the killer blow. Taking the ball waist-high following a corner-kick, Swinbourne turned near the penalty spot and hooked a left-footed shot wide of Sanders and into the net, near the post, Stuart Williams making a brave attempt to head the ball clear. Sanders then produced three excellent saves to deny Wolves further goals, and although Albion gave it a real go, they only managed a couple of late strikes on goal, and Bert Williams was equal to them both. Dudley and Kennedy worked themselves into the ground in a bold attempt to lift Albion, whose reserves simply couldn't match the professionalism and resilience of the Black Country seniors!

One suspects, although it will never be proven, that a full Albion team would not have lost this vital encounter. But they did and now Wolves, with this morale-boosting victory, were perhaps favourites to lift the title and so deny Albion the double. With this win

Albion 0

Wolverhampton Wanderers 1
Swinbourne

Albion v. Wolverhampton Wanderers

Bert Williams collects a high cross as Ray Barlow looks on.

Wolves moved up level on points with Albion (50 apiece) but were still in second place on goal-average. Race on.

Club News

On the same day as the Wolves game, Ronnie Allen and Johnny Nicholls both scored for England in a 4-2 win over Scotland at Hampden Park in a Home International match. The fixture also acted as a World Cup qualifier and was attended by a crowd of 134,544. The Scottish newspapers christened Allen and Nicholls 'The Terrible Twins'.

Physio Fred Pedley was busy treating no fewer than seven injured players as Albion manager Vic Buckingham started to scratch his head wondering what sort of team he might be able to field at Cardiff! Besides Messrs Rickaby and Heath, Frank Griffin (knee/ankle), Ray Barlow (leg), Johnny Nicholls (who was still struggling with his back), Gerry Summers (knee) and Reg Ryan (hip) were all causing some concern.

On 4 April 1954, Albion signed versatile defender Ron Bradley on amateur forms.

Albion: Sanders; S. Williams, Millard; Dudley, Dugdale, Kennedy; Cox, Ryan, Barlow, Carter, Cutler.

Wolverhampton Wanderers: Williams; Stuart, Pritchard; Slater, Shorthouse, Flowers; Smith, Broadbent, Swinbourne, Wilshaw, Hancocks.

ALBION SLIP TO THIRD SUCCESSIVE DEFEAT

Date: Saturday 10 April 1954
Location: Ninian Park
Attendance: 50,967

Match title: League
Referee: Mr J. B. Jackson (Watford)

Albion's frontline trio of Allen, Nicholls and Lee all came back for the trip to Cardiff. But Rickaby, Barlow and Griffin were noticeable absentees, and it was also confirmed that sadly Rickaby would miss the FA Cup final along with Heath. Cardiff, safe in mid-table, were playing for pride, while Albion needed to win to keep alive their hopes of achieving the League and Cup double. The biggest crowd for a club game at Ninian Park for almost a year saw an intriguing contest. Albion were far superior in terms of playing football to their opponents, but Cardiff had vast amounts of pluck and courage and matched the Baggies kick for kick during the first half, which saw Albion have eight shots at goal (four of them being seemingly easy chances, Lee and Allen both missing sitters with only keeper Ron Howells to beat) while City managed just three, Trevor Ford forcing Jimmy Sanders into a fine save from one of them.

In the forty-eighth minute Cardiff took the lead when Wilf Grant, looking at least a couple of yards offside, netted from close range after hesitancy in Albion's defence. Albion certainly missed the wing threat of Frank Griffin and the creative ability of Ray Barlow. Ford came close to adding a second for the Welsh side but Sanders denied the Welsh international again with a fine one-handed stop. As the minutes ticked by Albion pushed Reg Ryan (who was suffering from a damaged shoulder) and Jimmy Dudley forward a few yards, and for a quarter of an hour dictated play but failed to net an equaliser, Allen being the nearest with a right-foot shot from the edge of the area. Ryan was then injured and drifted out to graze on the left-wing – and with him went, realistically, any chance of winning the game. Cardiff, dangerous on the counter-attack, claimed a second goal on seventy-four minutes when Ford, getting the better of Joe Kennedy who earlier had received a nasty cut under his eye, beat Sanders with a wonderful header from a cross by the liveliest forward on the pitch, Tommy Northcott.

Albion tried to increase the tempo late on, but had it all to do, and although they perhaps had more possession in the closing stages, they lacked the killer touch in front of goal and in the end slipped to their third successive defeat – something that had not happened since December 1950. One supporter commented: 'Albion's hapless finishing let them down.' It was a long, sad journey back to the Midlands for the team and the huge contingent of supporters who had made the trip to South Wales to cheer on their favourites. Wolves capitalised on Albion's misfortune by beating Charlton Athletic 5-0 at Molineux to shoot to the top of the table, two points ahead of the Baggies (52-50).

Cardiff City 2
  Grant
  Ford

Albion 0

Club News

Albion chairman Major H. Wilson Keys, in his programme notes, stated that Albion had 30,000 applications from supporters (worldwide) for FA Cup final tickets. In the end the club received around 13,500 tickets (of all values) from the FA for the Wembley showdown with Preston North End.

Albion's Second XI lost 2-0 at home to Blackpool and slipped to fourth from bottom of the Central League.

On 12 April, Albion's youngsters lost the second leg of their FA Youth Cup semi-final clash with Manchester United at Old Trafford. They went down 4-0 in front of some 11,000 spectators to lose the tie 7-1 on aggregate.

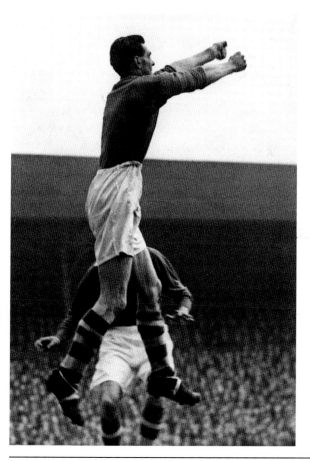

Cardiff City's Ron Howells punches clear as Albion try in vain to break through at Ninian Park.

Cardiff: Howells; Stitfall, Sherwood; Baker, Montgomery, Sullivan; Tiddy, Nugent, Ford, Northcott, Grant.

Albion: Sanders; S. Williams, Millard; Dudley, Dugdale, Kennedy; Cox, Ryan, Allen, Nicholls, Lee.

PENALTY WINNER FOR ALBION

Date: Saturday 17 April 1954
Location: The Hawthorns
Attendance: 38,742

Match title: League
Referee: Mr A. Brown (Middlesbrough)

Led out by skipper Len Millard, who was making his 500th first-team appearance for the club (including wartime) and his 350th in League and FA Cup competitions, Albion knew they had to beat Manchester City to remain in contention for the League championship and, indeed, the double. Manager Buckingham, somewhat relieved to have been able to field a full-strength side, saw his charges produce an unconvincing performance yet they managed to grind out a victory to earn themselves two vital points and at the same time register their sixth double of the season. The only goal of a rather scrappy encounter was scored from the penalty spot by Ronnie Allen after City's centre half Dave Ewing had handled the Albion centre forward's initial effort which was going into the net beyond keeper Bert Trautmann's right hand. Unfortunately, before and after scoring the decisive goal, the usually reliable Allen missed several chances and admitted afterwards: 'I think I left my shooting boots behind.'

In the opening few minutes George Lee and then Johnny Nicholls tested City's German-born goalkeeper. The visitors responded with a snap-shot from Joe Hayes which was off target. Ewing back-headed a Griffin centre to safety, and at the other end Jimmy Sanders pushed a Spurdle cross over the bar. Sounds exciting – but it wasn't! Referee Brown awarded the spot-kick in the 11th minute and Allen stepped up to drive his penalty right-footed wide of Trautmann's outstretched right arm with some power. Unfortunately Albion's defence did not inspire much confidence after that. Williams was given plenty to think about by the lively figure of Joe Fagan, and Jimmy Dugdale at times had his work cut out to contain the aggressive Billy McAdams. Jimmy Sanders, though, was solid enough between the posts while Millard, Jimmy Dudley and Ray Barlow gave their usual solid and sound performances, although the latter did lose the ball far too many times in centre-field. Before half-time Barlow fired in a 25-yard drive which Trautmann gathered at the second attempt; Allen mishit his shot from ten yards and Griffin's cross was only inches away from Nicholls' outstretched foot. Johnny Hart and Roy Paul tested Sanders and Williams somehow got in the way of a powerful shot from McAdams.

Play was meaningful for the first fifteen minutes of the second half before Albion, who were battling hard without making much impression and indeed were struggling to get their passing game together, launched two threatening attacks. Lee fired wide and Allen missed from eight yards. Late in the game both sides should have scored. For Albion, Allen's header was too near the keeper and his shot lacked direction; Nicholls fired outside a post and then put another effort over the top, while McAdams headed straight

Albion 1   **Manchester City 0**
    Allen (pen)

at Sanders before Fagan drove a shot into the side-netting when clear and bearing down on goal.

'In all games, a win is a win, especially in football. But this performance was one of Albion's worst of the season. Is the championship slipping away from them?' wrote one reporter.

Following the game it was thought that this might well be Buckingham's Cup final line-up, considering that the manager knew he would certainly be without the services of Heath and Rickaby (both injured). However, after gaining their first win since beating Port Vale in the semi-final, the team's overall performances would have to improve somewhat before the Wembley showdown with Preston, or the Baggies might just end up with nothing – and that would be catastrophic after such a wonderful campaign. Wolves drew 0-0 at Sheffield Wednesday, so the gap at the top (with just three games remaining) was down to one point in Wolves' favour: 53-52.

Club News

To mark the occasion of his 500th appearance for Albion, skipper Len Millard was presented with an inscribed tankard by former Baggies' right-winger Billy Elliott on behalf of the Supporters' Club.

The reserves lost again, beaten 2-0 by Barnsley at Oakwell. Albion's 'A' team was also defeated – 2-1 by Banbury Spencer in the Birmingham Combination Tillotson Cup.

Ronnie Allen beats Bert Trautmann from the spot.

Albion: Sanders; S. Williams, Millard; Dudley, Dugdale, Barlow; Griffin, Ryan, Allen, Nicholls, Lee.

Manchester City: Trautmann; Branagan, Little; McTavish, Ewing, Paul; Spurdle, Hayes, McAdams, Hart, Fagan.

POINT DROPPED AS ALBION WOBBLE

Date: Monday 19 April 1954   **Match title:** League
Location: The Hawthorns   **Referee:** Mr A. Murdoch (Sheffield)
Attendance: 45,972

Albion, unchanged after that vital win over Manchester City, found near-neighbours Aston Villa a hard nut to crack. And despite having most of the play in the early stages of the first half, and creating more chances at a ratio of three to one, they failed to bridge the visitors' defence in which former Baggies' amateur goalkeeper Keith Jones and centre half Frank Moss were both quite outstanding. Indeed, Jones saved well from Johnny Nicholls, Ronnie Allen (twice) and Frank Griffin while at the other end of the field Jimmy Sanders was rarely troubled, easily fielding one long-range effort from Johnny Dixon, and a header from Irish international winger Peter McParland.

As half-time approached, Albion's left-winger George Lee hit a thunderous drive which keeper Jones palmed over the bar. Griffin saw a right-footed drive from the edge of the 18-yard area pushed away by Jones and then Allen fired inches wide. At other end of the ground, McParland and then Johnny Dixon tested Jimmy Sanders.

It had been a surprisingly cleanly contested encounter, considering what was at stake from Albion's point of view. Albion deservedly took the lead in the forty-seventh minute. Nicholls, on the spot as usual and nipping past Moss, scored from five yards out after Jones had dropped Griffin's high cross at his feet. Villa came more and more into the game after this, and following two bright moves, they equalised through McParland in the sixty-second minute, following a mistake by full-back Stuart Williams. Albion's defence, now under severe pressure, held firm and gradually pushed Villa back. There were minor flurries in both goalmouths before the interval, and then immediately after the break Sanders thwarted McParland again while at the other end Nicholls and Lee had shots charged down. Thereafter it was nip and tuck for long periods, with neither goalkeeper unduly troubled, before Albion upped their game and went in search of a winner. With Villa defending desperately, Jones parried Griffin's low cross into the path of Nicholls, who duly banged the ball home, only to turn and see the linesman holding up his flag – a very close decision which caused an irate Baggies supporter to run onto the pitch and chase after the referee!

After George Lee, with a terrific left-footer, and Reg Ryan with a toe-poke from twenty yards had both tried their luck, the game fizzled out into a draw and Albion's championship hopes received another setback. Wolves were now the clear favourites to win their first ever League title. They made light work of beating Huddersfield Town 4-0 at Molineux in their fortieth match of the season to increase their lead over Albion to two points: 55-53.

Albion 1   **Aston Villa 1**
   Nicholls   McParland

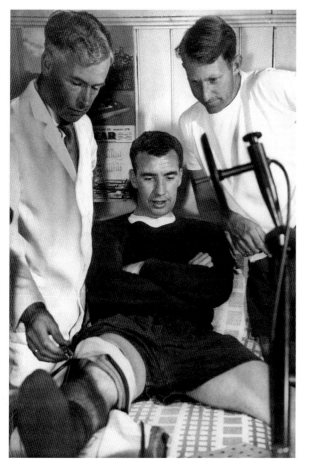

Left: Frank Griffin receiving treatment from club physio Fred Pedley for an injured right knee. *Above:* George Lee sent in one late thumping drive towards the Villa goal.

Club News

With games fast running out, manager Vic Buckingham had his entire first-team squad report to The Hawthorns early the following morning. There were no injury problems, although Frank Griffin was still feeling sore around his right ankle. With trainers 'W.G.' Richardson and Arthur Fitton present, a lot of talking was done and everyone knew that Albion had to win their remaining two matches if they were to stand any chance of claiming the League title. It was a tall order, considering that Wolves, two points clear and in the driving seat, were due to play Huddersfield (away) and Tottenham Hotspur (home).

Albion: Sanders; S Williams, Millard; Dudley, Dugdale, Barlow; Griffin, Ryan, Allen, Nicholls, Lee.

Aston Villa: Jones; Parkes, Aldis; Blanchflower, F. Moss, Baxter; K.O. Roberts, Tyrrell, Pace, Dixon, McParland.

DISASTER FOR DEMORALISED ALBION

Date: Tuesday 20 April 1954
Location: Villa Park
Attendance: 45,557

Match title: League
Referee: Mr A. Murdoch (Sheffield)

One could see and feel the tenseness in the Albion players when this game started – although no-one present inside Villa Park on a rather dull, chilly afternoon on a pudding of a pitch, could have believed, even contemplated, witnessing such a scoreline. Eric Houghton's team was placed below the halfway mark in the table, whereas Albion had everything to play for. Villa's pride was at stake, however, and the manner in which they began indicated that before Albion were going to be able to claim a victory, even take a point, they would have to prove they earned everything they got out of Villa Park.

Incredibly, Villa scored twice in the first ten minutes. After just ninety-five seconds Derek Pace converted McParland's low cross following a poor clearance by Williams, and eight minutes later Millard attempted to trap the ball near the left-hand post, and before he or goalkeeper Sanders could react, Pace nipped in to score with ease. A real gift!

After this early onslaught, Albion's defence broke up and collapsed so positively that almost every time Villa mounted a concerted attack, they got through to the last segments of Albion's resistance. Joe Tyrrell bagged number three on twenty-three minutes, and soon afterwards dived in front of Barlow and Dugdale to head home McParland's corner to make it four. Dixon cracked in another, and such was Villa's dominance that after just thirty-five minutes play the scoreline read Villa 5 Albion 0 – amazing.

In a rare Albion attack, Frank Griffin reduced the deficit before half-time (with a rare left-footer), but early in the second half Ronnie Allen was taken off on fifty-seven minutes with a groin strain, and future Villa player Jimmy Dugdale was switched to the left wing after taking a knock on the knee. Griffin was also hobbling on the opposite flank after aggravating his ankle injury.

In the second half the game degenerated into a crisp exhibition of shooting practice for Villa, and a colossal score was possible had it not been for the agility and skill of Albion's goalkeeper Jimmy Sanders, who certainly saved his colleagues from an embarrassing double-figure defeat! He saved magnificently from McParland, Tyrrell, 'Doc' Pace and Dixon as Villa stormed forward. Danny Blanchflower added a sixth goal late on with a 20-yard shot that deflected past Sanders off Barlow's head and soon after the Irishman struck a post. This was in fact the last real action and so ended Albion's ordeal.

A number of factors contributed, of course, to Albion's disaster. Villa's attack was a rejuvenated power, carrying only one man over twenty-two years of age, and which was altogether too fast and too sharp for Albion's tired-looking defenders. Furthermore, Albion

Aston Villa 6	Albion 1
Pace (2), Tyrrell (2)	Griffin
Dixon, Blanchflower	

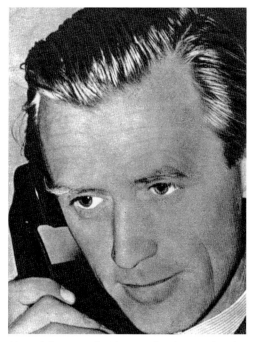

Above left: Vic Buckingham on the phone to his physio. *Above right:* Jimmy Sanders had no chance with at least three of the six goals.

seemed drained of all confidence after their series of recent setbacks and the psychological advantage was clearly with Villa. After this heavy defeat, Wolves were more or less declared League champions despite losing 2-1 at Huddersfield. With both clubs having just one game left to play, the Molineux men were two points ahead and had a far better goal-average.

Club News

Without hesitation physio Fred Pedley contacted manager Vic Buckingham and told him that he had ruled both Griffin and Allen out of Albion's final League game of the season at Portsmouth. He also suggested that Sanders should not be risked as he had jarred his wrist at Villa Park. Skipper Len Millard was also feeling a twinge behind his left knee.

It was announced that if the FA Cup final ended in a draw, the replay would take place at Goodison Park, Everton, on Wednesday 5 May (kick-off 6.30 p.m.). It would be an all-ticket affair with a capacity of 70,000. Albion and Preston would each receive 30,000 tickets.

Aston Villa: Jones; Parkes, Aldis; Blanchflower, F. Moss, Baxter; K.O. Roberts, Tyrrell, Pace, Dixon, McParland.

Albion: Sanders; S. Williams, Millard; Dudley, Dugdale, Barlow; Griffin, Ryan, Allen, Nicholls, Lee.

POMPEY CALL THE TUNE

Date: Saturday 24 April 1954
Location: Fratton Park
Attendance: 28,004

Match title: League
Referee: Mr J. C. Pollard (Cambridge)

Young goalkeeper Reg Davies was given his Football League debut at Fratton Park, while Grenville Jones and Wilf Carter replaced Griffin and Allen in the forward line. Albion, knowing full well that it would take a near miracle to win the title, played very well during the first half, creating a couple of chances and generally taking the game to Pompey, who in reply forced Davies into a couple of fine saves, while Jackie Henderson skimmed the bar with a 25-yard drive. Shortly before the half-time whistle George Lee signalled to the bench that he had pulled a muscle, and was immediately withdrawn.

Albion, with Lee back but limping badly, not surprisingly fell away after the interval and Portsmouth took control, scoring three times via Peter Harris (2) and Duggie Reid in the space of twenty-eight minutes. Harris broke the deadlock in the fifty-fourth minute with a smartly taken header – at which point Lee was immediately withdrawn for the duration of the game. After a Carter header struck a post, debutant Davies produced three magnificent saves to keep out efforts from Harris and Jackie Henderson, but he had no chance when Reid's 30-yarder flew past him on seventy-five minutes to make the score 2-0. With eight minutes remaining Harris raced clear and chipped delicately over the advancing Davies for Pompey's third. The Albion keeper, however, was doing wonderfully well and rescued his side with two more fine saves, while at the other end of the field Carter and Reg Ryan both went close to grabbing a consolation goal for Albion. Davies was applauded off the field at the end of the match after an excellent debut.

Wolves beat Spurs 2-0 to take the championship with a total of fifty-seven points. Albion finished runners-up, four points behind. Albion, in fact, won only two of their last ten matches, and in that time claimed just six points out of a possible twenty. In contrast, Wolves accumulated twelve points, winning five and drawing two of their last ten fixtures.

Club News

Albion's reserve side ended the season in eighteenth position with thirty-six points, twenty-two fewer than the champions Everton. They won two and lost four of the remaining six matches. Elfed Evans top-scored with twenty goals, followed by Wilf Carter with twelve. Billy Brookes appeared in thirty-eight of the forty-two matches, Harry Haddington in thirty-seven and Harold Wright in thirty-six.

Albion's youths took the runners-up prize behind Stoke City in the Midland Mid-Week League; the 'A' team finished tenth in the Birmingham Combination, the 'B' team claimed

---

Portsmouth 3
Harris (2)
Reid

Albion 0

thirteenth position in the Staffs. County League and the juniors were placed fourth in the Handsworth & District Junior League Division 1 (A).

As the preparations for the Cup final continued, it was announced that Albion's walking wounded would all be fit. The only problem Vic Buckingham had was who to play at right-back. Stuart Williams had not performed at all well since Stan Rickaby's injury and he was considering playing Joe Kennedy at right-back.

Albion's full allocation of tickets for the Wembley showdown was snapped-up within forty-eight hours of them going on sale, and every coach within a 25-mile radius of The Hawthorns was acquired by supporters, while sixteen special trains were also fully booked via British Rail for the big day out.

Wilf Carter deputised for Ronnie Allen at centre forward against Pompey.

Portsmouth: Dore; Wilson, Mansell; Gunter, Reid, Dickinson; Harris, Gordon, Henderson, Barnard, Dale.

Albion: Davies; S. Williams, Millard; Dudley, Dugdale, Barlow; Jones, Ryan, Carter, Nicholls, Lee.

The build-up to the FA Cup final

Sunday 25 April: The FA Cup final at Wembley was the major talking point throughout the Black Country as the countdown to the big day commenced in earnest. Albion had not played in an FA Cup final since 1935, and here, nineteen years on, they had the chance of lifting the trophy for the fourth time, having previously triumphed in 1888, 1892 and 1931.

Ronnie Allen was as nervous as anyone. He wrote in his book *It's Goals That Count*: 'Even the word Wembley has a wonderful sound to me, and the thought of actually playing on its beautiful turf was now in all our minds. There were no more matches to play now before the final, so no more injuries could interfere. Only now did the real excitement start to get into my bones. But how could we possibly hope to beat Preston on our form of the last few weeks?'

Indeed, Albion had played badly and lost, while Preston had done well, losing only once in six matches, and they were likely to be at full strength. Allen admitted that he wasn't 'very hopeful' of gaining a winner's medal ... but things were to change as the days ticked by.

Monday 26 April: The players reported to The Hawthorns for a fitness check. There was no training schedule but Frank Griffin, Ray Barlow, Reg Ryan, Allen and Joe Kennedy did some jogging and casual exercises before retiring for lunch with the rest of their colleagues at the Hawthorns Hotel.

Tuesday 27 April: Fifteen players reported to the ground at 10.30 a.m. for a final examination. There was a brief dressing room chat before everyone boarded the coach, waving au revoir to The Hawthorns' staff who would next see them in action at Wembley. The secret destination was at Twyford near Reading, arriving there in late afternoon. The party relaxed that evening before the real preparation work would begin. Said Jim Sanders: 'We had everything we could wish for – TV, radio, gramophones, magazines, newspapers, books – and it didn't take us long to settle in.'

After the evening meal, it was off to bed and early to rise!

Wednesday 28 April: After an 8.30 a.m. breakfast (some players had a full English, others just cereals and toast) it was off to the nearby Huntley & Palmer's recreation ground to commence strict training under the watchful eyes of Arthur Fitton and 'W.G.' Richardson. Manager Vic Buckingham, Freddie Cox, physio Fred Pedley and Harry Ashley were also in attendance. The first day's programme went down well and after a light lunch, a handful of players participated in a round of golf at the Sonning Golf Club, Reading. Johnny Nicholls, who had never played the game before, went along for fun, and saw his first tee-shot land in someone's

Confident and happy – Baggies fans setting off for Wembley.

Looking on as the flower-arranging takes place in front of the Royal Box where Albion's skipper Len Millard (fifth down) was to receive the Cup in twenty-four hours' time.

back garden. As he went to retrieve his ball, up popped a Great Dane! Nicholls quickly raced back to the fairway and said: 'I've retired from golf – it's too dangerous.'

After an excellent evening meal, most of the players relaxed in front of the TV while a few, including dab-hand Paddy Ryan, participated in a game of cards.

Thursday 29 April: After breakfast the party, now full of smiles, fit and ready for action, set off in glorious sunshine for a another training session, Fred Pedley reporting to his manager that everyone was 'one hundred per cent fit'. No one ventured out during the afternoon, the whole party choosing to relax in the lounge and gardens. Then, after an early evening meal, the players took part in a TV programme, together with their opponents, Preston, whereby they could ask 'Memory Man' Leslie Welch any sporting question they wished. No one could beat him – that is until he was asked: 'Who has the longest kick in football?' Welch admitted he didn't know. In fact, it was a catch question, as the answer was a Scottish goalkeeper who often kicked the ball to his team-mate whose name was Kilmarnock!

Friday 30 April: Sat at the breakfast table, with a little over thirty-two hours remaining before the final, one or two players had butterflies, Johnny Nicholls, Jimmy Dugdale and Ray Barlow included. It was at this time the manager announced his team: Sanders; Kennedy, Millard; Dudley, Dugdale, Barlow; Griffin, Ryan, Allen, Nicholls and Lee, the boss going for experience by naming Kennedy at right-back in place of Stuart Williams.

Another training session was staged between 10.30 am. and 12 noon, and everyone was amazed to see so many spectators present. The players did some jogging, a few sprints and casual arm and leg exercises, nothing strenuous. After lunch the team took a short boat trip on the River Thames before travelling to Wembley to have a look at the pitch and the stadium itself. As the players walked on the lush grass, Ronnie Allen halted near the penalty spot where the groundsman was adding the final touches of whitewash. Was it an omen? Then it was back to the hotel for another meal before followed by an early night in readiness for the big day. It had arrived!

Saturday 1 May: After breakfast, manager Buckingham got all his players together to explain the arrangements. There was no talk of tactics or of Preston's potential match-winner Tom Finney! That had all been done.

Frank Griffin recalled: 'The boss told us to play our accepted way; to go out and enjoy ourselves and then he simply ended by saying good luck to you all.'

Johnny Nicholls, the youngest player in the team and perhaps the most nervous, said: 'Two years ago I was playing in front of 1,000 people in reserve matches. I'm going to make the most of this day – and we're going to win.'

Lunch was taken at a country club just outside Wembley and then, with a police escort, the coach arrived at the stadium with time to spare. Dozens of telegrams were laid out on the dressing table, all of them wishing the team well. The tension was unbearable, but once the players had returned from the customary pre-match walk over the pitch, it was kit on, laces tied and down to business.

LATE GRIFFIN GOAL BRINGS ALBION CUP JOY

Date: Saturday 1 May 1954
Location: Wembley Stadium
Attendance: 99,852 (receipts £49,883, a record)

Match title: FA Cup final
Referee: Mr A.W. Luty (Leeds)

The two teams were presented to HM The Queen Mother prior to kick-off, and on a sunny afternoon, with the flags fluttering gently in a slight breeze, referee Arthur Luty from Leeds got the 1954 FA Cup Final underway at precisely 3.00 p.m., Ronnie Allen having the pleasure of setting the ball rolling after Len Millard had lost the toss.

Kicking into the sun, Albion, who were playing in their ninth final, thus equalling Newcastle's record, launched the first attack of the game down Preston's right, but the ball ran through to keeper George Thompson. Finney had his first touch of the ball in the fourth minute but was quickly tackled by Millard. Twice in the next two minutes the Preston winger went down inside the penalty area, but on each occasion play was waved on. The first shot of the match came from Jimmy Baxter, the Preston inside left who raced past Jimmy Dudley, but Jim Sanders watched his effort go safely past the right-hand post. Baxter then tried another shot (following Charlie Wayman's overhead kick), but this time the Albion keeper gathered the ball comfortably.

The captains meet – referee Arthur Luty watches Tom Finney (Preston) and Len Millard (Albion) shake hands before the start of the final.

FA Cup Final

Albion keeper Jimmy Sanders gets an early touch ahead of Bobby Foster.

In the first twelve minutes Preston defenders passed the ball back to their own keeper on five occasions, the last time causing Thompson some concern as Nicholls closed in fast. On the quarter-hour mark, trainer Arthur Fitton had to treat Allen for a bump on the head following Reg Ryan's throw-in, but the centre forward was quickly back into the action, heading towards goal after a decent centre from Nicholls. Nicholls then cut out Marston's intended pass for Docherty, but the Albion forward lost possession as he looked for a colleague. Nicholls was in action again on seventeen minutes. He collected Kennedy's pass and centred for Allen, whose header was saved under the bar by Thompson. After George Lee had tracked back to check Finney, and two Albion attacks had fizzled out, the deadlock was broken on twenty-one minutes. Preston centre half Joe Marston played the ball wide to his right full-back Willie Cunningham, who moved

Albion 3	Preston North End 2
Allen	Morrison
Griffin (2, 1 pen)	Wayman

upfield before striking his attempted clearance against the chest of Lee. The winger collected the ball, darted forward and crossed hard and low into the goalmouth where Allen, moving in smartly, side-footed home from close range.

Preston's reply was swift and decisive. Right half Tommy Docherty found space to cross the ball into the penalty area where outside left Angus Morrison, coming in on Joe Kennedy's blindside, headed firmly past Sanders for the equaliser, just fifty-five seconds after Allen's goal. Soon afterwards Wayman, with an acrobatic first-time kick, almost put Preston in front. Lee then raced through, and as Thompson came out to meet him, the winger fired over the top.

Albion, trying hard to exploit a weakness through the middle of Preston's defence, came close on two occasions in the twenty-sixth and twenty-ninth minutes, firstly through Lee (from a Nicholls pass) and then Nicholls himself, who just failed to get on the end of a superb long pass from Barlow. Kennedy was working hard at right-back and twice he stopped Morrison in his tracks as the winger attempted to go past him on the outside. Albion were certainly on top as the half-hour mark arrived, and Thompson dashed out to thwart Allen, climbing all over the striker to claim the ball. On thirty-four minutes, after Sanders had saved cleverly from Morrison's teasing left-wing corner, Allen was hurt again and Fitton once more had to use the magic sponge.

Finney, who had been very quiet up to now, had a chance of a break down the right, but Jimmy Dugdale's timely challenge ended the winger's progress. Griffin was next to threaten, but his cross was headed clear by Marston, and after the Albion right-winger had been fouled by Joe Walton, Lee skied Jimmy Dudley's free-kick over the bar. Then a smart one-two sent Ryan racing through but he was halted by Walton. Griffin and Lee both centred too near the keeper, and just before half-time both Docherty and Finney fired wide as Preston counter-attacked.

During the interval at least six players – Sanders, Dugdale, Griffin, Allen, Nicholls and Lee – all took a sniff of oxygen, and were immediately in the thick of the action when play resumed, Lee just running out of space as he chased a long ball from the irrepressible Ray Barlow, who was having a marvellous match. Finney got past Millard (for the first time) on forty-eight minutes but fouled Dugdale as it headed towards the danger-zone.

In the fifty-first minute, completely against the run of play, Albion found themselves behind. Flicking on Tommy Docherty's forward pass with Jimmy Dugdale in close attention, inside left Baxter sent Charlie Wayman clear of the Albion defence, but straightaway he looked at least a couple of yards offside as two Albion defenders committed the cardinal sin of standing still and appealing. The Preston centre forward ran on, rounded Sanders and netted with ease, thus preserving his record of scoring in every round. A disappointed Barlow held his head in his hands and beat his side to show his

---

Albion: Sanders; Kennedy, Millard; Dudley, Dugdale, Barlow; Griffin, Ryan, Allen, Nicholls, Lee.

Preston North End: Thompson; Cunningham, Walton, Docherty, Marston, Forbes; Finney, Foster, Wayman, Baxter, Morrison.

FA Cup Final

George Lee crosses from the left *(left)* and Ronnie Allen scores to give Albion a twenty-first minute lead *(below)*.

Opposite above: Preston hit back immediately and Angus Morrison heads in an equaliser.

Opposite below: Albion fall behind as Charlie Wayman, looking yards offside, taps in Preston's second goal.

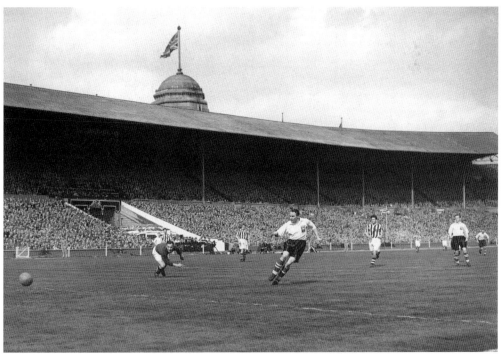

disappointment at the referee's (and linesman's) decision. The Albion left half said after the game: 'He was off and he knew it.'

Growing in confidence after this slice of good fortune, Preston pushed forward and Willie Forbes was injured in a strange fashion. He kicked at Nicholls' centre, sliced the ball behind for a corner and then collapsed holding his other ankle. The trainer was summoned onto the field to treat the left half-back. Barlow then floored Docherty with a powerful clearance before Thompson let slip a high cross, recovering just in time to prevent Allen from getting to the ball. Hands by Millard brought trouble to the Albion back line, but Sanders dealt comfortably with Wayman's ground shot following Finney's free-kick.

On 63 minutes Albion drew level via the penalty spot. After the ball had rebounded off Lee, Barlow, taking it in his stride, surged forward into the left-hand side of the area where he was floored by a clumsy challenge from Docherty. Referee Luty had no hesitation in

Ronnie Allen cracks home his penalty to bring the scores level at 2-2.

Preston's goalkeeper goes up for a high cross as Johnny Nicholls tries to get in a header.

pointing to the spot. However, as Allen went to place the ball down, he noticed that a large divot had been removed from the centre of the spot (someone had driven their heel into the ground), so he positioned it fractionally off-centre. The referee, however, made him replace the ball. So, as cool as you like (I think) Allen duly replaced the divot and the ball, walked back, turned, ran up and with his right foot struck a hard and low shot to Thompson's right. The keeper got his hand to the ball but couldn't prevent it from entering the net: 2-2.

Finney was sent sprawling on the edge of the Albion 18-yard box a couple of minutes later: no foul. And then, taking a brilliant pass in his stride from Lee, Barlow got to the byline and from his low cross, Walton was fortunate not to concede an own goal, Thompson just managing to tip the ball round the post. It was end-to-end stuff, and after Thompson had made a grand leap to clear Griffin's cross, Millard raced fully fifty yards to intercept a crossfield pass aimed for Finney. Nicholls almost caught the Preston defence napping when he followed up a long through ball from Dudley and was hurt as he fell over the keeper. He had to go behind the goal to receive treatment, returning to see Morrison head a Finney corner high over the bar. With 15 minutes to go the tempo slowed. Finney's tame shot flew two yards over the crossbar and at the other end Allen's

FA CUP FINAL

Frank Griffin watches his shot squeeze past keeper Thompson for Albion's winning goal.

The keeper's on his knees as Albion's George Lee jogs away to celebrate victory!

Albion skipper Len Millard gleefully receives the FA Cup from HM The Queen Mother.

Ready for that lap of honour.

FA Cup Final

Hip hip hooray for the winners!

Match-winner Frank Griffin kisses his lucky boot as Ray Barlow and Ronnie Allen congratulate the winger.

Len Millard gives his speech at the celebration dinner after the victory.

25-yard snap-shot was easily dealt with by Thompson. A sharply struck shot by Morrison was touched round a post by Sanders and from the corner Foster headed wide.

With three minutes to go – and extra time looking a strong possibility – Albion scored a dramatic winner. Kennedy and Ryan linked up down the right before Griffin headed the ball past Walton and sprinted clear. He cut into the penalty area and was almost on the byline before he fired in a hard and low shot, the ball finding the net under the diving body of Thompson. What a finish. The ball was hoofed as far down the field as possible by Albion after that. They weren't going to lose now – and when the final whistle sounded the delight on the players' faces was a picture to behold. A delighted and joyful Len Millard proudly climbed the thirty-nine steps leading to the Royal Box where he gleefully collected the trophy from the Queen Mother. Jimmy Dudley, behind him, accepted his medal with the plinth. The Albion supporters roared their approval as the captain held the coveted trophy aloft.

What they said ...

Frank Griffin, the match-winner: 'I didn't think I had a chance when Reg Ryan nodded it down to me. And I still think that Thompson made a mistake in letting it through. He dived far too late.'

Skipper Len Millard: 'It pays having a look at Wembley before the final. Our lads walked over the pitch on Friday to get to know the feel of the ground – and we won. Preston didn't bother to go along at all.'

Ronnie Allen: 'I felt like crying when Frank (Griffin) scored his solo winner. Collecting that winners' medal was the proudest moment of my life.'

Reg Ryan: 'We didn't need the luck of the Irish – we played very well and deserved our victory.'

Joe Kennedy: 'What a day ... I never believed I would be a Wembley Cup winner when the season started. It was a great, great occasion.'

George Lee: 'I knew we would win – I felt it my bones. Frank's winner came at the right time – they were deflated when the goal went in – we weren't.'

Jimmy Sanders: 'I was nervous to start with but quickly brushed away any fears of losing. We were going to win – for Stan [Rickaby] and Norman [Heath].'

Ray Barlow: 'In my opinion it was a nasty foul. I might not have scored a goal, but I certainly would have reached the ball if Docherty hadn't brought me down.'

Manager Vic Buckingham: 'I knew the lads would do the business. Prior to the game I said that if we could produce anything like our best form then we would have no trouble in beating Preston. I know it was close in the end, too close for comfort really, but victory was sweet – and we deserved it, especially after the disappointment of missing out on League honours. I though the whole team played superbly well – I was proud of them all.'

Tom Finney (Preston captain, speaking at the Savoy Hotel, London): 'All credit to Albion. They played well, were organised and certainly their football was better than ours. I felt the penalty was harsh – perhaps obstruction would have sufficed. It's a bitter pill to swallow, losing a cup final.'

Regarding the penalty decision, referee Arthur Luty said: 'Docherty came straight across Barlow and never intended to play the ball. It was definitely a foul and therefore a penalty was awarded.'

Arthur Fitton (Albion's trainer): 'It's a good job I got Jimmy Dudley's arm away from Frank (Griffin) after his winning goal. He was throttling him in the excitement; Frank almost passed out – but what a day, what a win.'

Author and Midlands journalist Peter Morris wrote in his book *Soccer In The Black Country*: 'To win the Cup was no more than Albion deserved ... It was a personal triumph for manager Vic Buckingham, the dedicated visionary who had forged this fine side together from almost the rawest of materials.'

Maurice Smith (*The People*) started his post-match report with the words: 'My Lords, Ladies and Gentlemen: I give you a toast to the team who never gave up. To eleven great fighters in white and blue. To the men who won the Cup: West Bromwich Albion.' Later he wrote: 'I though Dugdale had a great game; Kennedy and Millard too ... I never saw Nicholls play better ... Thrust and counter-thrust – what a game.'

Cyril Chapman (*Birmingham Gazette*): 'It was a great triumph over adversity, for not only did Albion surmount those recent misfortunes which had brought an inevitable loss of confidence, but they overcame the loss of an early lead and then, when their opponents drew ahead, pressed in pursuit so spiritedly that they were able to regain lost ground and finally, right on the finishing line, to thrust forward first against the tape.'

Roy Peskett (*Daily Mail*): 'It was not a classic game, but the goals and the controversy made it all very exciting and a match to remember.'

Charles Harrold (*Sports Argus*): 'A street ahead but victory by a neck ... Any other result would have been a tragedy for Preston's goal was so clearly offside that a gasp went up all round that end of the ground.'

Peter Wilson (*Daily Mirror*): 'Albion were, in my mind, the better team. They played the better class of football, looked more decisive when going forward and created more chances.'

Stan Halsey (*Sunday Pictorial*): 'Preston relied too much on Finney.'

Gil Merrick (Birmingham City & England goalkeeper): 'There was no shadow of doubt in my mind that Albion were the better football team; they pulled together as a team and played football as a team – and Reg Ryan was my man of the match for his tremendous hard work.'

My father: 'You'll never forget that, son – I knew we would win. That was great, and what about Ronnie ... he's some player, isn't he?'

For the record

The gate receipts from the Final – £49,883 – were divided thus: Albion: £6,894 15s 10d; Preston: £4,524 14s 2d; entertainment tax (including band): £13,000; FA Cup pool: £6,500; Football Association: £6,500; match expenses, hire of Wembley Stadium, police costs, insurance, referee/linesmen's fees, etc.: £12,462.

The eleven Albion players, the team manager and trainer each received a winner's medal plus £20; the Preston players were rewarded with runners-up medals only.

The clubs were also allowed to share among their players the following talent money: Albion £550 for winning the Cup and a further £440 for being League runners-up. Preston received £440 for being Cup runners-up.

All ninety-two Football League clubs that took part in the 1953/54 FA Cup competition each received £1,000 (from the FA Cup pool).

Club news

Following their triumph at Wembley, Albion's official Cup-winning celebration dinner was held at the Café Royal, Regent Street, London W1, where the champagne fizzed all night!

Among the guests who mingled with the 1954 players and club officials were many former Albion players, including Jesse Pennington who skippered the team in the 1912 Cup final; nine more stars from the 1931 FA Cup-winning team who joined 'W.G.' Richardson, namely Harold Pearson, Bert Trentham, George Shaw, Bill Richardson, Jimmy Edwards, Tommy Glidden, Joe Carter, Teddy Sandford and Stanley Wood; Jimmy Murphy and Wally Boyes from the 1935 final team (beaten by Sheffield Wednesday) and Blackpool's Stan Mortensen who scored a hat-trick v. Bolton in the 1953 final.

On the Sunday evening the party watched the BBC Television programme *What's My Line*.

When they returned to the Midlands with the Cup on the Monday after the final, more than 150,000 supporters assembled along the five-mile route from Birmingham's Snow Hill Station to the centre of West Bromwich. When they arrived at the town hall there were 25,000 fans there to greet them.

On 9 May, Albion's reserve full-back Stuart Williams was capped by Wales against Austria in Vienna.

Johnny Nicholls and Ronnie Allen played for England vs Yugoslavia in Belgrade on 16 May. The home country won 1-0. Also on 16 May, Jimmy Dugdale lined up for England 'B' against Yugoslavia 'B' in Ljubljana. Again, the home side won 2-1.

A week later (23 May) Dugdale, Allen and Johnny Nicholls (as a second-half substitute) all figured in the England vs Switzerland 'B' international in Basle, and once again they were on the losing side, this time by 2-0.

Manager Vic Buckingham kept his full forty-man professional squad for the 1954/55 season, although eleven of the players would be involved in National Service duty for part of the campaign.

Ready for the triumphant homeward journey – boarding the train in London destined for Birmingham with the FA Cup.

Showing the coveted trophy to their delighted supporters en route to West Bromwich Town Hall.

The vast crowd outside West Bromwich Town Hall, awaiting the arrival of the players and the Cup.

Above left: Playing staff retained by manager Vic Buckingham for the 1954/55 season. *Above right:* Len Millard, Jimmy Sanders and Johnny Nicholls with the silver pot.

Members of the 1953/54 squad pictured at a fortieth anniversary reunion at The Hawthorns in 1994.

Players and management

Ronnie Allen, born in the Potteries in 1929 and signed from Port Vale for £20,000, spent eleven years with Albion (1950-61) before transferring to Crystal Palace. A wonderfully gifted footballer, he scored 234 goals in 415 first-team games for the Baggies and won five England caps. He later managed Albion (and several other clubs abroad). Allen died in 2001, aged seventy-two.

Ray Barlow, a tall, elegant and highly-skilful left half, who also occupied five other positions for Albion, spent sixteen years at The Hawthorns (1944-60) during which time he appeared in 482 first-team matches and scored forty-eight goals. He was capped once by England. Born in Swindon in 1926, he now lives in Pedmore, Stourbridge.

Billy Brookes, reserve to Barlow, was an Albion player for eleven years (1947-58), making twenty senior appearances. Born in Dudley in 1931, he now resides in Lichfield.

Albion's reserve forward Wilf Carter was born in Wednesbury in 1933 and was a player at The Hawthorns from 1949 to 1957. He scored twelve goals in sixty-one outings before moving to Plymouth Argyle and later assisting Exeter City. He now lives in Bath.

Reading-born Freddie Cox was winger with Arsenal and Tottenham Hotspur before joining Albion as player-coach in 1953, reaming at the club for three seasons. He scored once in four senior outings for the club. Cox died in 1973.

Reg Cutler, a Blackheath-born left-winger and George Lee's deputy, spent six years with Albion (1950-56) before moving to Bournemouth and later playing for Portsmouth and Stockport. Now sixty-eight, he made five first-team appearances and currently lives near Wolverley, Kidderminster.

Reserve goalkeeper Reg Davies, a native of Tipton (born in 1933) was an Albion player from 1949 to 1955 and made four League appearances before moving to Walsall, later serving with Millwall, Orient and Port Vale. He now resides in Tipton.

Right half Jimmy Dudley first signed for Albion in 1944 and over the next fifteen years amassed 320 senior appearances and netted eleven goals. He then had 175 games for Walsall. Born in Glasgow in 1928, he is now living in Great Barr.

Jimmy Dugdale, born in Liverpool in 1932, made seventy-five appearances for Albion (1950-56) before transferring to Aston Villa, with whom he won a second FA Cup-winner's medal. He is now living in Stechford, Birmingham.

Cup final hero Frank Griffin, born in Manchester in 1928 and now resident in Shrewsbury, scored fifty-two goals in 275 appearances for Albion between 1951 and 1959. He joined the club from Shrewsbury Town and on leaving The Hawthorns signed for Northampton Town.

Norman Heath, sadly injured at Sunderland, started his Albion career in 1942. He went on to appear in 169 games before his retirement in 1955, after which he was forced to work for a living under severe handicap. In April 1956 Heath received the proceeds of a testimonial game between Albion and an International XI at The Hawthorns – an expression of thanks by the club and supporters for his indomitable courage in adversity. Born in Wolverhampton, he was only fifty-nine when he died in Birmingham in 1983.

Ken Hodgkisson, reserve inside forward, played for Albion from 1949 to 1955 and thereafter for Walsall. He scored four goals in his twenty-one outings for the club, and later played in more than 350 games for the Saddlers. Born in West Bromwich in 1933, he still lives locally.

Reserve right-winger Grenville Jones, born in Nuneaton in 1932, made three appearances for Albion during his eight years with the club (1947-55). He later appeared in 276 games for Wrexham. He died in 1991.

Born near Whitehaven in 1925, Joe Kennedy was a superb centre half who played 397 times for Albion (scoring four goals) between 1948-61. Signed from Altrincham, he moved to Chester from The Hawthorns. He died in West Bromwich in 1986.

George 'Ada' Lee was a dashing outside left who netted sixty-five goals in 295 appearances for Albion over a period of nine years, 1949-58. Formerly with his home town club York City, he was signed from Nottingham Forest and later returned as Albion's trainer. He died in 1991, two months before his seventy-first birthday.

Long-serving skipper Len Millard, who developed into a very sound left-back, appeared in 627 first-team games for Albion (477 at competitive level) during his twenty-one years with the club (1937-58). Born in Coseley, he died in 1997, aged seventy-eight.

Johnny Nicholls, the 'Poacher', was born in Wolverhampton in 1931 and scored sixty-four goals in 145 competitive games for Albion who he served from 1950 to 1957. An England international (two caps) he moved to Cardiff City and later played for Exeter. He died in 1995 when driving home from an Albion match.

Right-back Stan Rickaby, now living in Perth, Australia, made 205 appearances for Albion (scoring two goals) between 1950 and 1955. Born in Stockton-on-Tees in 1924, he joined the club from Middlesbrough, won one England cap and later became an accountant.

Irish international wing half/inside forward Reg Ryan scored thirty-one goals in 272 appearances for Albion between 1945 and 1955. He later played for Derby County and Coventry City. He won a total of seventeen full caps and died in Birmingham in 1997, aged seventy-one.

Goalkeeper Jimmy Sanders, a fighter pilot in the Second World War, spent eleven years at The Hawthorns between 1945 and 1956, during which time he appeared in 391 first-team games. He moved to Coventry City and later assisted Hinckley. Born in London in 1920, he sadly died in 2003.

Reserve full-back Stuart Williams joined Albion from Wrexham in 1950, and after making 246 appearances and scoring nine goals he moved to Southampton in 1963. He later returned to The Hawthorns as trainer, seeing Albion win the FA Cup again in 1968.

A sheet of autographs featuring the 1953/94 squad.

Now living in Southampton, he won thirty-three caps for Wales (the most by an Albion player).

Manager Vic Buckingham played most of his football as a full-back with Tottenham Hotspur. He was boss at The Hawthorns from 1953 to 1959 and also managed Ajax, Sheffield Wednesday, Fulham, Seville and Barcelona.

Trainer/coach 'W.G.' Richardson was a great marksman for Albion between 1929 and 1945, netting 328 goals in 444 first-team matches. An FA Cup and promotion winner in 1931, he gained one England cap (vs Holland in 1935). He died in 1959, aged forty-nine.

Trainer/coach Arthur Fitton, another former player, occupied Albion's left wing during the period 1922-32, playing in the same team as Richardson (above). Born in Leicestershire in 1902, he also served with Kidderminster, Manchester United, Preston and Coventry and later worked as a warden in Kinver. He died in 1984.

Fred Pedley was a senior physiotherapist with Albion during the 1950s and later did a similar job with Aston Villa. He is still living in West Bromwich.

Harry Ashley, assistant trainer, was a reserve at The Hawthorns from 1934 to 1937, returning to play as a guest for Albion during the Second World War when he scored six goals in thirteen games. He also played for Derby County and Darlington.

Players' records

Name	League Apps	League Goals	FA Cup Apps	FA Cup Goals	Totals Apps	Totals Goals
Ronnie Allen	39	27	6	7	45	34
Ray Barlow	39	5	6	1	45	6
Billy Brookes	2	-	-	-	2	-
Wilf Carter	5	-	-	-	5	-
Freddie Cox	4	1	-	-	4	1
Reg Cutler	1	-	-	-	1	-
Reg Davies	1	-	-	-	1	-
Jimmy Dudley	42	1	6	1	48	2
Jimmy Dugdale	32	-	6	-	38	-
Frank Griffin	38	6	6	1	44	7
Norman Heath	34	-	5	-	39	-
Ken Hodgkisson	5	1	-	-	5	1
Grenville Jones	2	-	-	-	2	-
Joe Kennedy	13	-	1	-	14	-
George Lee	41	7	6	-	47	7
Len Millard	40	-	6	-	46	-
Johnny Nicholls	38	28	6	4	44	32
Stan Rickaby	33	1	5	-	38	1
Reg Ryan	36	7	6	1	42	8
Jimmy Sanders	7	-	1	-	8	-
Stuart Williams	10	-	-	-	10	-
Opponents	-	2	-	1	-	3
Totals	**462**	**86**	**66**	**16**	**528**	**102**

Only Jimmy Dudley appeared in all 42 League and 6 FA Cup ties during the season.

Albion manager Vic Buckingham fielded the following team (in League and Cup action) on sixteen occasions: Heath; Rickaby, Millard; Dudley, Dugdale, Barlow; Griffin, Ryan, Allen, Nicholls, Lee.

Attendance statistics

The average League attendance at The Hawthorns in 1953/54 was 38,279 (the aggregate for twenty-one matches was 803,852). This was the biggest since 1948/49, when the average was 38,819.

The best single turnout was that of 53,210 for the visit of Blackpool on Saturday 20 March 1954, while the lowest was 20,306 against Preston North End on Saturday 2 January 1954.

Away from home, Albion's average (twenty-one matches) was 41,256 (aggregate 866,382).

The biggest away crowd was 56,590 at Molineux for the clash with Wolves on Saturday 14 November 1953, and the lowest was that of 17,144 at Middlesbrough for the Wednesday afternoon game on 24 February 1954.

Albion's overall League average (home & away) was 39,768 (an aggregate for forty-two matches of 1,660,283).

Albion's four home FA Cup ties attracted an aggregate of 195,673 spectators at an average of 48,918.

For all six Cup games in 1953/54, Albion's average attendance was 60,624 (an aggregate for six matches of 363,746).

For all games at The Hawthorns in 1953/54 (total twenty-five) Albion's average attendance was 39,981 (an aggregate of 999,525) and for all away games (total twenty-three, including two Cup games) the average was 45,063 (an aggregate of 1,033,503).

In 1953/54 Albion played a total of forty-eight League and FA Cup games and the average attendance at each one was a club record 42,374 (aggregate 2,031,028).

Fact file

Ray Glazzard (the Huddersfield Town centre forward) topped the Division One scoring charts with twenty-nine goals; Albion's Johnny Nicholls was second with twenty-eight and Ronnie Allen third with twenty-seven.

Allen, with a total of thirty-four goals in League and cup was Division One's overall top marksman. Only three Division Two players, John Charles (Leeds United) with forty-three, Bedford Jezzard (Fulham) with thirty-eight and Arthur Rowley (Leicester City) with thirty-six, scored more goals during the season that the Albion centre forward.

Only Ipswich Town, with twelve in Division Three (South), and Port Vale, with ten in Division Three (North), recorded more away wins than Albion. Wolves (Division One) and Brighton & Hove Albion (Division Three (South)) also notched nine victories on the road.

Albion's 7-3 triumph at Newcastle United was their biggest win in League football (home and away) since April 1949 when they defeated Bradford Park Avenue 7-1 in a Division Two game at The Hawthorns. It was also the first time Albion had bagged seven goals in an away League game since beating Newport County 7-2 at Somerton Park in a Division Two match in September 1946.

The 6-1 defeat at Villa Park on 20 April 1954 was, in terms of goals conceded, Albion's heaviest in League football since September 1951 when they lost by the same score at Burnley.

Albion were undefeated in their first nine League matches; lost only one of their first fifteen and in that time won six in succession away from home. Later in the season (between 25 December 1953 and 6 March 1954) Albion remained unbeaten in ten League games (it was fourteen in all up to 13 March, including four FA Cup ties).

Albion completed the double over six teams: Huddersfield Town, Manchester City, Manchester United, Preston North End, Sheffield Wednesday and Tottenham Hotspur. They also beat Preston North End and Spurs in the FA Cup. Only two clubs, Portsmouth and Wolves, achieved the double over Albion.

Albion scored at least one goal in thirty-five of their forty-two League games and failed to find the net in just two home matches (v. Burnley in a 0-0 draw and Wolves in a 0-1 defeat).

The team netted 102 goals in total – eighty-six in the League and sixteen in the FA Cup.

Albion's 100th goal of the season was scored by Ronnie Allen against Preston North End in the FA Cup final at Wembley, on 21 minutes.

Albion used a total of twenty-one players during the course of their League programme – the second-lowest number since 1932/33, when they used eighteen. In season 1952/53 they utilised twenty.